Staying
in Demand

Staying in Demand

How to Make Job Offers Come to You

C. D. Peterson

*FEATURING 94 ACTION STEPS
FOR CAREER SELF-RELIANCE!*

McGraw-Hill, Inc.

New York   San Francisco   Washington, D.C.   Auckland   Bogotá
Caracas   Lisbon   London   Madrid   Mexico City   Milan
Montreal   New Delhi   San Juan   Singapore
Sydney   Tokyo   Toronto

Library of Congress Cataloging-in-Publication Data

Peterson, C. D. (Carl D.)
    Staying in demand : how to make job offers come to you / C.D.
Peterson.
        p.   cm.
    Includes index.
    ISBN 0-07-049655-2   —   ISBN 0-07-049656-0 (pbk.)
    1. Career development.   2. Self-culture.   3. Self-presentation.
4. Job offers.   I. Title.
HF5381.P474   1993
650.14—dc20   93-9791
                                                       CIP

1 2 3 4 5 6 7 8 9 0   DOC/DOC   9 9 8 7 6 5 4 3

ISBN 0-07-049655-2 {HC}
ISBN 0-07-049656-0 {PBK}

*The sponsoring editor for this book was James H. Bessent, Jr., and the production
supervisor was Donald Schmidt. It was set in Baskerville by North Market Street
Graphics.*

Printed and bound by R. R. Donnelley & Sons Company.

 This book is printed on recycled, acid-free paper
containing a minimum of 50% recycled de-inked fiber.

To Odessa, Wendy, Stephanie, and Chris

Contents

Acknowledgments   xv

Part 1. A Reality Check   1

Introduction   3

The best economic insurance you can buy is having skills that are in
demand and having lots of employers, headhunters, and other
influential people know *who* you are, *where* you are, and *how good*
you are.

1. The New Realities of Employment   7

Layoffs, cutbacks, the background, and the new factors of employment. Downward mobility, personal obsolescence, boredom,
burnout, the demise of employment loyalty, and the end of single-
company careers.
   The new *good* news, and the need for self-reliance.

ACTION STEP 1   *Understand What Happened to Loyalty
                 and Job Security   8*
ACTION STEP 2   *Understand What's Going on Today   9*

Part 2. Consider *All* Your Options   19

2. Own Your Own Job—Four Entrepreneurial Options   21

Corporate employment is declining. People are trading in their
jobs to go into business. Not all are trading willingly; the cutbacks

and mass layoffs occurring in companies throughout the country are forcing it. Mergers, foreign competition, and just plain cost reduction have stripped the security out of having a corporate job.

ACTION STEP 3   *Take the "Entrepreneurial Quiz"*   22
ACTION STEP 4   *Learn the Four Routes to Ownership*   25
ACTION STEP 5   *Examine in Detail How to Start a Business*   26
ACTION STEP 6   *Explore Consulting*   29
ACTION STEP 7   *Check Out Franchises*   37
ACTION STEP 8   *Consider Buying an Established Business*   42

3. Consider Your Conventional Employment Options   47

The greatest number of options for most people exists in the world of conventional employment; working full-time for monetary compensation.

ACTION STEP 9   *Examine "In-Placement," i.e., Reemployment within Your Present Company*   47
Substep 9.1   Stay Where You Are   47
Substep 9.2   Consider Promotion, Demotion, and Sidestepping   49
Substep 9.3   Restructure Your Job or Create a New One   50
ACTION STEP 10   *Examine "Out-Placement," i.e., Employment Options Outside Your Present Company*   50
Substep 10.1   Do the Same Job in a Different Setting   50
Substep 10.2   Take on a Different Job   51

4. Consider Some (Slightly Offbeat) Alternative Employment Opportunities   53

Maybe a full-time, full-pay company job isn't for you. Maybe corporate demand for your knowledge and skills has evaporated. You have alternatives. Part of staying in demand is knowing how to locate special—some might say offbeat—opportunities.

ACTION STEP 11   *Remember the Armed Services*   54
ACTION STEP 12   *Understand Bartering*   54
ACTION STEP 13   *Consider Care-Giving*   54
ACTION STEP 14   *Work on Contract*   54
ACTION STEP 15   *Be a Courier or Chauffeur*   55
ACTION STEP 16   *Down-scale*   55
ACTION STEP 17   *Try Flextime*   55
ACTION STEP 18   *Serve in Government or Charities*   56
ACTION STEP 19   *Work in Government*   56
ACTION STEP 20   *Work at Home*   56
ACTION STEP 21   *Become an Independent Contractor*   57
ACTION STEP 22   *Moonlight*   59

ACTION STEP 23 *Work Part-Time* 59
ACTION STEP 24 *Don't Shun Personal Service* 59
ACTION STEP 25 *Contemplate Religious Service* 59
ACTION STEP 26 *Retire!* 60
ACTION STEP 27 *Seek Seasonal Employment* 60
ACTION STEP 28 *Become a Seminar Leader* 61
ACTION STEP 29 *Explore Teaching* 61
ACTION STEP 30 *Try Temporary Work* 61
ACTION STEP 31 *Volunteer* 62

Part 3. Reinvent Yourself—Invest in Yourself 63

5. Reinvent Yourself as Your Own "Personal Enterprise" 65

Your self-reliance depends first on your ability to produce value competitively. Whether you work for a company, own your own business, or engage in any of the alternatives in Chapter 4, your efforts must yield something which the market wants and which is of higher value than the market could buy somewhere else.

ACTION STEP 32 *Learn How Employment Value Is Determined by Employers* 65
ACTION STEP 33 *Learn How Demand Changes* 69
ACTION STEP 34 *Start with What You Have—Conduct a Personal Assessment* 71
    Substep 34.1 Find and Overcome Your Weaknesses; Find and Exploit Your Strengths 72
    Substep 34.2 Know the Limitations of Personal Assessment 76
ACTION STEP 35 *Find Your Life Values—Do What You Love* 77
    Substep 35.1 Zero in on Your Passion 78
    Substep 35.2 Integrate Your Passion with Your Career Plan 78
    Substep 35.3 Conform Your Passion and Practicality 80
    Substep 35.4 Get Help Pursuing Your Passion 81
ACTION STEP 36 *Set Your Goal* 81
ACTION STEP 37 *Build a Career/Life Plan to Establish Your Earning Power* 81

6. Self-Invest to Build Your Employment Value 83

Secretaries once honed their dictation and typing skills, then they mastered word processing. Soon they will be learning the skills to exploit the new CD Interactive technology.

Drafters once mastered tedious drawing skills. Tomorrow, instead of designing parts and then assemblies, these technicians will create, view from different perspectives, and even operate complete machines that don't yet exist. It's called *simulation/animation*.

If you don't know what CD Interactive technology is, or if you haven't already thought about how to use a video camera to feed images into your computer, you may learn from your competition and should consider your personal enterprise at a competitive risk.

ACTION STEP 38   *Commit Yourself to Never-Ending Education and Training*   84

ACTION STEP 39   *Decide What You Are Now and What You Want Your Employment Value to Be*   84

Substep 39.1   Devise a Self-Investment Strategy That Balances Expertise with Flexibility   84

ACTION STEP 40   *Become an Expert, Totally Focused*   84

ACTION STEP 41   *Become a Generalist, Stay Flexible*   85

ACTION STEP 42   *Achieve Balance between Flexibility and Expertise*   85

ACTION STEP 43   *Develop Yourself as an Economic Resource; Choose a Mix of Hard and Soft Skills*   86

ACTION STEP 44   *Develop a Plan to Acquire the Knowledge and Skills You Want*   91

ACTION STEP 45   *Pursue Skills Acquisition through Institutions*   92

ACTION STEP 46   *Take Advantage of Work-Related Training*   93

ACTION STEP 47   *Apprentice Yourself to an Expert, Formally or Informally*   94

ACTION STEP 48   *Gain Knowledge and Skill on Your Own*   94

ACTION STEP 49   *Get Help with Your Development Plan*   96

ACTION STEP 50   *Recognize That It's All up to You*   96

Part 4. The Subtle (and Not-So-Subtle) Art of Self-Promotion

97

7. Get Sharp! Get Recognized! . . . and Make Job Offers Come to You!

99

You need to have in-demand skills for your personal enterprise to succeed. Good work habits and job performance are also necessary elements for success. They are *necessary*, but they are *not sufficient* to guarantee your self-reliance.

To repeat: The best economic insurance you can obtain is having skills that are in demand *and having lots of employers, headhunters, and other influential people know* who *you are,* where *you are, and* how good *you are.*

ACTION STEP 51   *Learn the Basic Techniques of Job Search*   99

Substep 51.1   Establish Objectives   100

Substep 51.2   Respond to Advertisements   100

Substep 51.3   Convert Actions to Accomplishments and
Experience to Results   100
Substep 51.4   Contact Recruiters   101
Substep 51.5   Contact Companies Directly   101
Substep 51.6   Network—But with Care   102
ACTION STEP 52   *Employ a New Strategy for Today's Market—
The Targeted Résumé "Job Proposal"*   103
ACTION STEP 53   *Don't Stop When You Find a Job*   103
ACTION STEP 54   *Learn to Promote Your Personal Enterprise*   104
ACTION STEP 55   *Prepare to Promote*   109
ACTION STEP 56   *Initiate Your Own Performance Review*   109
ACTION STEP 57   *Understand What Others Want and Expect*   110
ACTION STEP 58   *Milk Meetings for All They're Worth*   110
ACTION STEP 59   *Make Organizational Membership a Platform
for Getting Known*   111
ACTION STEP 60   *Assume Leadership in Organizations*   111
ACTION STEP 61   *Work at Everyday Communications and
Social Activity*   111
ACTION STEP 62   *Cultivate a Genuine Interest in Others*   112
ACTION STEP 63   *Get Involved in Political Activity*   112
ACTION STEP 64   *Take Part in Charity and Other Volunteer
Work*   112
ACTION STEP 65   *Get Quoted*   113
Substep 65.1   Have Something Worth Quoting   113
Substep 65.2   Find Out Who Might Quote You   114
Substep 65.3   Make Sure Those Who Might Quote You Know
about You   114
ACTION STEP 66   *Write Articles (or Even Letters) That Get
Noticed*   115
ACTION STEP 67   *Provide High-Visibility Pro Bono Consulting*   116
ACTION STEP 68   *Become a Lecturer*   116
ACTION STEP 69   *Create or Participate in Seminars*   117
ACTION STEP 70   *Develop and Teach Courses on Your
Specialty*   118
ACTION STEP 71   *Create, Conduct, and Publicize Surveys*   118
ACTION STEP 72   *Give Gifts, Mementos, Books, etc.*   119
ACTION STEP 73   *Clip and Send Articles of Interest*   119
ACTION STEP 74   *Publicize! Promote Your Family, Pets, Home,
Food, Hobbies, Clothes, Travels, and More*   120
ACTION STEP 75   *Use Targeted Audience Networking*   120
ACTION STEP 76   *Master Memorable Introductions—
"The Two-Minute Drill"*   122
ACTION STEP 77   *Create Your Own Self-Promotion Network*   122
ACTION STEP 78   *Integrate Your Self-Promotion Activities*   123

Part 5. Creating Security for Your Personal Enterprise

ACTION STEP 79   *Prepare Yourself for Possible Unemployment or Self-Employment*   126
ACTION STEP 80   *Assemble a Team of Advisers*   126
  Substep 80.1   Don't Become a Hostage to Your Advisers' Expertise   127

8. Develop Your Legal Strategy

It comes as a surprise to people that others can launch legal attacks which must be defended regardless of the merit of the argument. It comes as a greater surprise that arguments of little or no apparent merit can be successful. "The uncertainties of litigation" is an oft-used phrase that describes well the sometimes capricious behavior of courts, judges, and juries. While there is no guaranteed way to avoid legal entanglement for your personal enterprise, there are precautions and initiatives you can take.

ACTION STEP 81   *Conduct a Review of Your Legal Situation*   129
ACTION STEP 82   *Construct the Elements of Your Legal Strategy*   130
ACTION STEP 83   *Choose a Legal Form for Your Personal Enterprise*   131

9. Develop a Financial Strategy

Financial security is both a goal and a measure of self-reliance. Oddly, though, many of us treat our financial status as a residual of all our work—what's left over from our income after we spend what we want or must, and scramble to save what we can. We may do a pretty good job of making individual financial decisions, but we have no cohesive strategy to achieve financial security.

ACTION STEP 84   *Set Financial Objectives and Strategies*   138
ACTION STEP 85   *Set Your Income Objective*   138
ACTION STEP 86   *Protect Yourself from Loss*   139
ACTION STEP 87   *Plan for Your Accumulation of Wealth*   147
ACTION STEP 88   *Plan for Your Retirement*   148
ACTION STEP 89   *Conduct Tax and Estate Planning*   156

10. Develop a Personal Wellness Strategy

Your *personal* enterprise is built on one and only one foundation—you.

ACTION STEP 90   *Guard Your Personal Safety*   159
ACTION STEP 91   *Practice Preventive Health Care*   160

ACTION STEP 92   *Get Exercise and Rest*   161
ACTION STEP 93   *Choose What You Eat and Drink*   161
ACTION STEP 94   *Put Some Balance in Your Life*   162

Conclusion   **163**

Appendix A.   Self-Promotion Matrix   **165**

Appendix B.   The Health Test   **169**

Appendix C.   Personal Life Cycle   **179**

Index   181

Acknowledgments

Ideas for books are a dime a dozen. What turns an idea into a finished (and hopefully useful and interesting) book are the motivations and help visited on the writer.

My motivation stemmed from my work with people in "outplacement," a polite term for those who have lost their jobs. These fine people were, almost universally, ill-equipped and unprepared for their situation. If only they had explored the idea of attaining career self-reliance, their lives could have been much better. I hope this book helps all working people and prevents at least some of them from facing the gut-wrenching experience of being without a way to earn a living.

My help came from several sources. First and always is the help my family gives me in many ways, large and small.

Attorney Fred Baker of Baker, Moots and Pelligrini practices law in Danbury, Connecticut. He reviewed the legal section of the book and provided up-to-date advice.

Dr. Brian Schwartz of Greenwich, Connecticut and New York City consults on career matters. He consulted with me on the section devoted to personal appraisal and added a useful structure to it.

Mr. John Durkin of Financial Underwriters in Danbury, Connecticut provided much-needed advice on personal finance and the excellent examples of retirement calculations.

Finally I want to acknowledge my agent, Peter Elek, and my editor at McGraw-Hill, Jim Bessent, both of whom believed in this book even though it did not fit into a neat category. It isn't a "résumé" book or a "job search" book, or a "self-help" book.

The three of us decided the book is about self-reliance, and we call it a "survival" book.

C. D. Peterson

PART 1
A Reality Check

Nothing can bring you peace but yourself.
Nothing can bring you peace but the
triumph of principles.

RALPH WALDO EMERSON
essay on "Self-Reliance"

Introduction

*There is a time in every man's education
when he arrives at the conviction that envy
is ignorance; that imitation is suicide;
that he must take himself for better, for
worse, as his portion . . .*

RALPH WALDO EMERSON
essay on "Self-Reliance"

The best economic insurance you can buy is having skills that are in demand and having lots of employers, headhunters, and other influential people know *who* you are, *where* you are, and *how good* you are.

Companies have changed the way they manage employees and their jobs, but employees—people—have not changed in response.

If you were caught up in one of the tidal waves of layoffs, cutbacks, and downsizings that swept through the 1980s, chances are you were made to feel part of a significant event. Maybe your company president made an announcement. Surely a team from your human resources department was deployed to cushion the blow and, in many cases, introduce you to an outplacement firm which would help you find another job. If your company or the layoff was important to the community, it probably made the papers.

That was then, when downsizing was a singular event. Today things are different. Cutting and redeploying people are now integral parts of day-to-day management as companies recognize and respond to the ferocious nature of world competition. What was once an event is now common practice.

People feel helpless. They worry. They hope and wish things were more secure. But they don't do much except wait, or maybe look for another job where, once again, they will worry and feel helpless.

Working people must now see themselves as personal economic enterprises, almost like human factories or businesses whose task it is to generate income and create personal wealth and security for themselves. Like corporate businesses, these human versions need investment (training) and marketing (promotion) to keep producing income over a lifetime. The goal is self-reliance.

Staying in Demand—How to Make Job Offers Come to You, offers two fully developed components in a program to help you gain control of your working life and create security for your personal earning power.

1. *Become more valuable by building your employment value.* Layoffs and cutbacks are now common business strategies as companies strive for competitiveness, so upgrading skills and knowledge must become your strategy. The foundation for recognition is to have real value. You are your own basic economic resource. Invest in that resource.

   - Find out what your company and your boss want.
   - Find out what other employers want.
   - Learn what skills will be wanted in the future.
   - Decide what *you* want.
   - Review the alternatives: self-employment, changing jobs, changing careers, part-time, flextime, moonlighting, etc.
   - Develop new skills, become an expert, get experience.
   - Use educational opportunities, get on project teams.
   - Build a career/life plan to establish your earning power. Practice *self-investing.*

   Staying in Demand provides how-to steps for each one of these elements.

2. *Gain recognition of your employment value.* Systematic, continual self-promotion is the best insurance policy you can buy. You can't afford to *hope* others will know about you. You can't afford to *wait* until you're fired to begin. You must *take action* to be recognized.

- Maintain a list of who should know about you: the boss, co-workers, other bosses, headhunters, consultants, industry members, professional associates, civic club members, charitable organization members, alumni, friends, neighbors, classmates, media people, bankers, auditors, customers, suppliers, even competitors.
- Use the basics of getting recognized: networking, organizational membership, attendance at meetings and conventions, social contact.
- Learn the professional aspects of getting recognized: assuming leadership of organizations, getting quoted, writing articles (or even letters) that get you noticed, pro bono consulting, lecturing, participating in seminars, teaching, conducting surveys, and more.
- Form your own PR network where members will act as a public relations company for each member.

Self-promotion must become a lifetime activity to insure your recognition in the marketplace and to counteract the loss of security from employment. Don't wait until you are without a job and forced to join the pack as they mass-mail résumés, chase the want ads, and network frantically.

Being self-reliant does not mean being the "lone ranger." Strategic alliances, support groups, and even an employment relationship may all be part of your strategy of self-reliance. Self-reliance means financial and physical self-reliance, too.

Financial self-reliance means providing your own safety net of insurance, savings, and retirement, and having a bare bones budget ready to put in place if needed.

Staying in Demand makes this observation: *You will probably be unemployed or self-employed at sometime in your working life. You need to protect yourself from economic disaster by staying prepared.*

- Learn how to control your financial obligation "nut."
- Set baseline insurance coverages.
- Find private (individual) coverage sources.
- Understand the uses of incorporation.
- Understand the uses of independent contractor status.

- Provide for retirement on your own.
- Earn concessions from employers by having your own benefits.

Good health is essential for your enterprise to function. Preventive maintenance with exercise and other good health habits is analogous to maintaining the assets of any business.

A career was once like a chess game, with known moves and rules, but today it's more like a frightening, quick-reflex, video game with unexpected, often random, twists and turns. A mistake can mean the game—your career—is over.

Earning a living and creating security in the 1990s cannot depend solely on the old ethic of "do a good job and you'll have a good job." Doing a good job is still a must, but it's no longer enough. In the 1990s you will have to acquire new skills, gain new experiences, and adapt to new demands.

But even more important, *you* will have to take the initiative to determine what those new demands and skills are and *you* will have to make sure that employers and others know that you have them.

It's that kind of self-reliance that *Staying in Demand—How to Make Job Offers Come to You* tries to provide.

You, as your own personal enterprise, are the lifelong resource you must develop and market to earn income and build wealth.

1

The New Realities of Employment

The self-reliant person can always find or create bright spots to be sure. But there is a purpose in painting a realistic picture early in this book, as I do in Chapter 1. That purpose is to create in you the realization that you cannot entrust your life and your future to the institutions and practices that have existed since the end of the great depression. They served us well, but a new century will require new perspectives. The final decade of this century will be the forge to fire the individual human determination which that new century will test. The material presented in Chapter 1 is based in fact, and it is not so much doomsaying as it is a description of the very real changes that are taking place in the economy and the workplace.

The decade of self-reliance began in 1990. Corporations have abandoned paternalism and cast off any traces of obligatory loyalty. Government help at all levels is shrinking. International competition respects only economic strength and vigor. As in America's early days, each of us needs to kindle a pioneering spirit of rugged individualism. It's going to be up to you to take care of yourself and your family, to be self-reliant.

Organizations will continue to be the major source of employment and, after these big waves of downsizing, they will slowly stabilize as the baby boomers begin to retire at the end of this decade and a shortage sets in. Being self-reliant and working as a team member inside an organization are not in conflict. A good team player is also reliant.

ACTION STEP 1 *Understand What Happened to Loyalty and Job Security*

Before we learn what it will take to be self-reliant in the nineties, we need to have a common understanding of the forces that have shaped the dilemma we now face and a common awareness of how portentous is the problem to be solved.

For some this will be old and sad news, but they can take heart that their plight is recognized, and grab any means for self-reliance that this book might provide them.

For others this will be new and startling news, and that's good because they need to have strong motivation to do the work to become self-reliant.

The Background. When World War II ended, America was the world's sole economic power with undamaged, newly built industrial plants and unchallenged, freshly developed technology. The GI Bill sent millions of middle-class people to college, while government policies and loan programs fueled a housing (and baby) boom from Levittown to Long Beach.

The Eisenhower years brought billions of dollars for highways and bridges, giving us jobs and a new infrastructure. America was strong and secure at mid-century.

From Strength to Weakness. But strength led directly to a new phenomenon. Our strong dollar was being spent overseas as new competitors, fresh from rebuilding their war-ravaged businesses, were aggressively challenging us in our own markets. In the 1960s the balance of payments shifted and we became net importers.

In 1971 the exchange rates were allowed to float and the dollar fell. Although this made U.S. goods easier to sell, it made the now very large flow of imported goods more expensive to buy, and prices crept up. The oil crises arrived and by the mid-seventies inflation was at a full gallop. At first, corporate profits benefited from inflation. Companies granted expensive and self-perpetuating cost-of-living formulas for wage increases. Because these and other cost increases could easily be passed on by raising prices, investments in capital and technology to improve efficiency and productivity were neglected.

The 1980s brought little but financial market legerdemain, creating only temporary service jobs, debt, and a few millionaires.

From Security to Jeopardy. Near the end of the 1980s it was observed in a *Business Week* article:*

> Companies became trapped in the worst of all possible worlds. By the late 1970s even though profits still seemed strong, productivity growth was slowing to a crawl. The competitiveness of American manufacturers, as measured by their share of world markets, was sagging. The Federal Reserve Board pushed up interest rates to fight inflation, and the dollar soared. American companies had to cope with higher credit costs while being priced out of markets overseas and surrendering big chunks of their domestic markets to cheaper and better imports.
>
> [In the late 1980s] The adjustment has been painful. Plant closings, layoffs, restructuring, mergers, and acquisitions have provided the "leitmotiv" of the corporate drama for at least five years. Some industries have undergone wholesale elimination of excess capacity in a process of consolidation designed to carve up a shrinking pie among fewer companies.

In the five years since that article, things have worsened. Layers of managers, thousands of workers, and much of the cadre of financial services hires have been laid off as companies face the ferocity of international competition against world standards of quality, price, and value.

ACTION STEP 2 *Understand What's Going on Today*

Now, unless you take action, it's you, the individual, who can be trapped in the worst of all possible worlds, with threats to your paycheck coming from many sides.

Your company's programs to improve productivity and lower costs cause layoffs in the short term. The president and CEO of Data General announced on a national news show† that his company's improvements in manufacturing processes now allowed the firm to shrink from 5 million square feet of space to 2 million square feet and still produce the same number of products. He foresaw more

---

* *Business Week,* October 5, 1987.
† CNN, November 12, 1991.

and more layoffs, not only for his firm, but others in his industry, as productivity improvement becomes an ongoing process, not an occasional event.

These so-called structural layoffs usually result in a migration of people to new jobs in new industries or locations. But this time an insidious recession is wringing out jobs everywhere, often permanently.

Entrepreneurs aren't immune as they, too, report fewer orders and lower levels of business. Because they don't typically contribute to unemployment insurance, they are particularly exposed during downturns.

Even the U.S. Army is reducing its work force, using civilian techniques of offering packages and seeking volunteers, but resorting to more coercive tactics of withholding reenlistment contracts when needed.

New Factors This Time Around

> This is not a blip caused by a recession. This is a historic restructuring of the U.S. work force that's taking place over many years.*

Americans have weathered employment contractions before. In the past, business cycles seldom hit all businesses at once and ways were found to prime the economic pump. Today the economy faces a banking crisis which this time does impact a greater proportion of businesses. The economy labors under huge governmental debt which limits its ability to intervene, though a modest program to rebuild Eisenhower's 40-year-old infrastructure has been undertaken.

Federal government insolvency and, in some cases, policy have sucked up funds previously destined to flow into state treasuries and the programs they supported. The layoff of state workers—even state police and state university employees (unheard of in times past)—has become commonplace. State programs aimed at social, welfare, medical, and other such services are under severe pressure.

As we might expect, the financial pressure at the state level has been leveraged down to the local level. Local budget meetings have become contentious and commonly divisive affairs pitting young parents against the elderly, environmentalists against businesspeo-

---

* Dan Lacey, editor of *Workplace Trends,* Associated Press, December 21, 1991.

ple, and eventually neighbor against neighbor. In my own county, local budgets in several towns were rejected three and four times until cuts were made in such previously sacred accounts as teachers' salaries and school programs. These rejections occurred at packed town meetings traditionally attended by few residents.

Below the Cracks—More Cracks.   While some resources have been directed to improving our plants, productive methods, and infrastructure, new problems demand attention.

Insolvencies among companies and their insurers have put pension funds at risk. You may know some retirees who never conceived of such a situation who are facing the prospect of poverty as they are trapped between reduced or dried-up pensions and rising medical costs.

Rising health-care costs are forcing firms, unable to offset or pass on the increases, to shift the added cost to employees. These copayments and higher deductibles can strip hundreds of dollars a month from your paycheck.

Savings and loans, banks, and even the fund created to save them continue to weaken. State governments furlough massive segments of their operations, cutting services to their economies and wages to their employees.

Maybe more ominous than all these things are the tears showing up in our social fabric.

Topics like immigration, protectionism, welfare reform, and job quotas are back in the limelight. These are issues of income redistribution, of recutting the economic pie to favor one group over another to achieve some degree of desired equity. These are issues that arise when that pie is stagnant or shrinking. They are also those which divide the country and add no value to its wealth.

The stagnant economy and job shrinkage is being blamed for such diverse problems as the emergence of extremist politicians, the extraordinary level of child poverty and the upsurge in street gangs.

Finally, it has not escaped notice that the income of Americans is becoming redistributed. The rich are getting richer and the income gap is widening. The richest 5 percent of the population has seen its after-tax, after-inflation income grow 60 percent over the last 15 years while the bottom two-thirds of the population watched its real income *decline* by worse than 10 percent.

Changing Perspectives/New Expectations. We are marking a watershed in American life as the prospect of ever-rising prosperity has come to an end. No longer can each generation automatically look forward to better jobs, bigger homes, more leisure, and greater security. In fact, only one generation in our country's history, the generation which matured in the 1940s, enjoyed the explosive growth in opportunities that we have recently witnessed.

To the dismay of today's young and the sadness of their parents, younger generations will be lucky to live nearly as well as their forebears.

Periodicals are full of stories about people from the middle class who are facing daily strains of survival. The business section of the *New York Times** detailed the agony of families "Trapped in the Impoverished Middle Class" where even a modest life is slipping away. *Business Week†* first told of people who ". . . don't have enough money to walk through the mall," and then devoted a cover‡ to "Downward Mobility."

As early as mid-1991 *The Wall Street Journal* reported that U.S. living standards were slipping, and had begun the slide even before the recession. An autumn of political denial failed to overcome popular intuition and daily experience, eventually putting this momentous condition in the center of American focus.

Check out the story of Susan Balee in Figure 1-1.

Most individuals have bet on the system. A good education brought to bear with solid work habits is supposed to guarantee the good (and most likely better) life. For over 10 years the system that said "do a good job and you'll keep a good job" has been changing to one that says "I can pay you if you can solve my problems, lower my costs, or increase my income—if I have room for you."

Managements applied this primal philosophy openly, and some would say ruthlessly, even to their own top-level executives: at Westinghouse, Goodyear, IBM, the White House. . . . When executives in these organizations were terminated, the usual soft-peddling of the reason for dismissal wasn't there. Management made no bones about the fact that the executive did not perform.

* *New York Times,* November 17, 1991.
† *Business Week,* October 21, 1991.
‡ *Business Week,* March 9, 1992.

One Individual's Reality

One poignant story is that of Susan Balee, a well-educated woman who, as she put it, "commits the crime of poverty." With her last $170, Ms. Balee goes to court to pay a ticket for driving with an expired registration. After observing a procession of defendants receive various measures of justice, she receives her fine of $167.50 only to learn from the cashier that the fine schedule had been increased to $203. Flirting with the top limit of her credit card, she manages to draw the needed cash and pay the fine. Her feelings:

> I went to court feeling self-righteous, but I left feeling humble. It used to be that there was a wide margin between me and the majority of the people who were called to that courtroom. But suddenly it seemed that there was very little difference between us at all. I had an education, but I couldn't get a decent job with it. I was married, but my husband was forced to live in another state for his job, and I was forced to raise my daughter without his help. I could still say "Have credit card, will travel," but how long would it be before I would have to abandon even that motto? How long before I couldn't afford to make the minimum payments? I was a member of the well-educated middle class, but I felt the cracks beginning to open beneath my moccasins. It wouldn't be that hard to slide into the underclass—a few bad months and we could fall through the cracks.*

* *Northeast*, the *Hartford Courant*, October 6, 1991.

Figure 1–1. The story of Susan Balee.

Downward Mobility. In the early eighties many of us chronicled stories of shocked senior and middle-level executives who were experiencing unexpected joblessness. Television and print news did in-depth pieces on some of these new unemployed and introduced readers to "downsizing" strategies, "outplacement" companies, and "networking" techniques.

Now, in the early nineties, there are stories about the enormous stress gripping some of these same people as they face joblessness a *second time*, further in debt, older, and with deeply diminished confidence.

The American Management Association reported that the 12-month period ended June 30, 1991 was the worst period for job cutting in history. Though individual cuts were smaller, more companies pursued downsizing. For the first seven months of 1992, staff cuts ran 2.3 percent ahead of 1991.

White-collar workers are receiving most of the publicity in this period because it's the first time they have been in the unemployment lines and in line for food stamps, but blue-collar workers aren't exempt. General Motors alone used a variety of incentives to encourage 12,000 workers to leave and is still pushing for more, possibly as many as 74,000. General Electric and others are using similar programs.

Facts from the Bureau of Labor Statistics* show many of the jobless don't recover. Even in the good times of the eighties as many as 14 percent never found work. Those that did were reemployed at an overall *decrease* in wages of 11.8 percent. In addition, 25 percent of those reemployed took cuts of 20 percent or greater and 25 percent lost health insurance. Not counted as unemployed are another 11 percent who were full-time workers but who are now part-time, self-employed, or unsalaried in a family enterprise.

The Plight of the Employed.   Those who are employed face problems. Tough times have created a whole new cadre of business celebrities—the tough-minded managers. Gone are the charismatic CEOs who inspired us and the fast-food franchise kings who showed us how simple success could be. The covers of magazines today feature the grim faces of managers who "cut fat to the bone" and who are "fighting a struggle for survival" as they consolidate, merge, scuttle sick operations, and shed workers.

As these leaders install this new culture into their businesses, and as other firms copy their model, the American worker who *is* employed is paying a price in higher stress and lower job satisfaction.

Lower Job Satisfaction.   The abrupt stop of the growth elevator of the eighties caused many people to bang into the ceiling. For some, the economic brake had the added drag of discrimination. For many, the vision of the firm providing them increasing responsi-

* *Business Week,* September 16, 1991.

bilities, more varied and interesting assignments, and ample opportunity to grow and to experience personal fulfillment became dim. Deficient positive expectation coupled with negative concerns about basic job security have led to widespread dissatisfaction.

The *Harvard Business School Bulletin* of April 1991 contains a lengthy article about graduates of their school who are dissatisfied with their careers and the substantial consulting activities now devoted to helping such people seek fulfillment through various techniques of career transition.

This growing unhappiness has contributed to a continuing wave of entrepreneurship and to books with titles like *Is Coffee Break the Best Part of Your Day?** and *Staying Up When Your Job Pulls You Down.*†

Stress. Confronting dissatisfaction, a basic thrust of this book, connotes some power of action. Enduring stress, however, connotes a wearing away of health and well-being, a sapping of the power necessary to effect change.

The most obvious source of stress on working people is the fear of losing their jobs. This chapter has so far painted a grim picture of employment prospects, one which is being reinforced at this writing by IBM's announcement of 20,000 more planned layoffs.

No longer protected by past service, loyalty, or recognized accomplishments, employees experience the stressful frustration and fear of economic impotence, the feeling of helplessness.

Economic impotence undermines all feelings of personal financial security. Commonly adding to the stress is the crushing load of personal debt. Credit card borrowing and extended car loans have stretched borrowers to the limit, only a few paychecks from insolvency.

In a particularly harsh turn of events, the single most important asset of most Americans has, for some, become a nightmarish liability. Spurred by the seemingly endless prosperity of the eighties and the attendant soaring house values, owners borrowed heavily against the bloated equity in their homes, taking on heavy second-mortgage payments. Now, with job loss a real possibility, and as they see or hear of others losing their homes to foreclosure, these borrowers know it can happen to them, and the stress builds.

---

* Dick Leatherman, Human Resource Development Press, Amherst, Mass., 1990.

† Joanne Bodner and Venda Raye-Johnson, Perigee Books, New York, N.Y., 1991.

Another kind of stress is gripping working people: the more familiar but now more pervasive stress of time pressure. Cutbacks by and large have focused on people, not the work they do, so the employees who remain after a cutback, in addition to worry and any guilt, must now carry a heavier work load.

Fax machines, voice mail, pagers, and the like have wiped out the luxury of turn-around time and out-of-pocket time. Because these devices have been installed in hotels and resorts, vacations no longer will let you "get away from it all." It all stays with you.

International business with its time differences means doing business at all hours, and frequent international travel has long been known as a source of stress.

One specific manifestation of stress is the increase in sleeping disorders. Dr. Neil B. Leavy, Director of Colombia Presbyterian Hospital's Sleep Disorders Clinic, said in a *New York Times** article, "When people start losing their jobs or fearing they might lose their jobs, they start losing sleep."

The loss of sleep leads to depression, which hurts job performance, which puts the individual in further jeopardy of being terminated.

And Now for the Good News . . .   As a way to make a point, this chapter has intentionally painted a bleak picture of the economy, corporate America, political futility, and the specter of this country's first generational maelstrom of downward mobility.

But good news can still be found. Consolidations and mergers may make the subsequent U.S. entities better able to compete with our larger international rivals.

The IRS has approved rules which allow employers to make pension contributions weighted toward older workers, helping them retain and attract these experienced people.

Notable business leaders are making early calls for others to rebuild the sense of loyalty that once existed between employer and employee. Joseph P. Mack, chairman and CEO of Saatchi & Saatchi Advertising, warns managers:

> But with neither corporations nor employees loyal to each other, the result is a reduction in individual productivity, greater on-the-job anxiety, unwillingness to take risks and a weakening of the entrepreneurial spirit—all signs of trouble.*

* *New York Times,* November 10, 1991.

One powerful piece of good news can remove worries a employment "doomsday" scenario. The work population in t is declining, and that means a labor shortage looms in the latte. half of this decade. Even with weak employment, the underlying labor force is growing at only one-third the rate it did after previous downturns began.

The record-breaking cutbacks have barely nudged up the number of unemployed actively seeking work. You may be puzzled by the fact that with weak employment and the publicized massive layoffs, the unemployment rate has remained fairly constant around 7 percent. Job seekers who just drop out account for some of the relief on the rate but perhaps a more important factor is the passing of the surge in baby boomers and women who entered the work force for the first time in the 1970s and 1980s.

Many of today's job seekers with in-demand skills are able *and do* turn down less-than-great jobs. Others are able to bargain with employers and trade money for more free time, which is a growing desire among dual-wage-earning families.

As an example of what in-demand skills can mean to you, 1992 graduates of several schools who took masters degrees focused on the latest manufacturing engineering techniques, were swamped with offers and were able to command salaries as high as $90,000. For skilled minorities and females, it's actually a sellers' market in the midst of recession.

Some firms are implementing programs to retain skilled workers. *The Wall Street Journal*[†] reports that Reebok, enjoying success throughout the period, seeks to retain managers by offering them training in skills they need to excel. "Even in a recession there is no shortage of job opportunities for highly skilled people," a Reebok official said.

Entrepreneurs with marketable ideas, sharp skills, and solid determination are still starting businesses and profiting from their efforts and risk taking. Dell Computer is prospering by deftly implementing customer-sharp strategies. Trucking deregulation has spawned nearly 30,000 new companies since 1980.

The good news in this chapter is that highly skilled people are always in demand, and that those who can develop and match their

---

[*] *New York Times,* December 15, 1991.

[†] *The Wall Street Journal,* November 12, 1991.

knowledge and experience to the changing needs of the market-place will have skills with earning power and can afford to be choosy about how to make a living even in a recession.

The other good news is that if you can afford to wait, there will be jobs aplenty as demand curves up over supply.

But if you can't afford to wait until the next century, if you want more control over your life, if you want more satisfaction from earning income and building wealth, then please read on and learn how to take the initiative to build and promote your personal economic value *now*.

PART 2

Consider *All* Your Options

*The voyage of the best ship is a zigzag line
of a hundred tacks. See the line from a
sufficient distance, and it straightens itself
to the genuine tendency. Your genuine
action will explain itself, and will explain
your other genuine actions.*

RALPH WALDO EMERSON
essay on "Self-Reliance"

Before trying to experience the sense of power and control that
comes from taking action, we need to explore what action or
actions will be right for you to take with regard to your work life.
Not only is it comforting, in a way, to know what they are, but it
is also true that you will get better results if you plan well.

Part of your planning should involve sifting through all the
options available to any person trying to build his or her demand
in the workplace. You might be surprised at some of the topics
covered in this next section. But by giving these topics your
serious consideration, you will begin to crystallize in your mind

what course you really want to take, and you will strengthen your hand in all subsequent career-related moves by knowing more clearly just how many choices you *do* have.

You can't, then, be pressured just to accept the first offer that comes along, and the improved perspective will keep you out of unsatisfying situations by building your resistance to the doomsayers.

The spectrum of options ranges from having a job to buying a franchise to teaching to retiring to much more. You can work full-time, part-time, or flextime. You can be a temp or an interim employee. With the new electronics, you can be at a company, in a shared office, or at home. You can moonlight. You can be an independent contractor. You can volunteer for community service or run for election to give public service. You can change jobs, change companies, change location, change careers, and change skills.

The options also include issues of lifestyle, personal values, and fundamental goals.

This section will describe the options, organized into *entrepreneurial ownership, conventional employment,* and *alternative employment.*

2
Own Your Own Job—Four Entrepreneurial Options

Over a million people started their own businesses last year—that's double the rate of past decades. Another 3½ million people bought businesses.

While all this entrepreneurship is occurring, corporate employment is actually declining. Why are more people trading in their jobs to go into business? We have already covered the most visible reason: They're not trading; the cutbacks and mass layoffs occurring in companies throughout the country are forcing it. Mergers, foreign competition, and just plain cost reduction have, as noted, stripped the security out of having a corporate job.

Adding to the problem is the huge bulge in population called the *baby boom*. The people in that bulge are now adults and are crowding the promotion ladder at the very time and place that cutbacks are occurring.

Some positive reasons drive this entrepreneurial surge, too. *The personal computer* is one positive force. These powerful tools have become more affordable and easier to use. Entrepreneurs handle tasks and take on challenges formerly reserved only for large companies, and they do most tasks in their homes.

Franchises have made entrepreneurship easier, more affordable, and less risky. Franchises are experiencing explosive growth. Estimates are that by the year 2000 half the retail sales in the U.S. will be through franchised outlets. With their packaged programs of systems and other support, franchises are ideal for the first-time business owner. They let people be in business "for themselves but not by themselves." Franchises are now available in more types, sizes, and prices than ever.

Network groups are another, more recent, positive force for entrepreneurship. These "tips clubs" are springing up everywhere. Some are very formal; some are more like social mixers. The objective is to get a group of businesspeople together on a regular basis strictly to make business contacts.

Finally, while not a new reason, the American desire for *independence and self-reliance* is still a most powerful motivator to have a business of your own.

Before looking at this option it's important to remove a well-publicized myth, the myth of the "entrepreneurial type" or personality.

> *There is no entrepreneurial personality, no special set of traits, which ensure success or guarantee failure. You are as able as the next person to explore the entrepreneurial alternative.*

Tests show it. Entrepreneurs are as varied as any of us. Of course good work habits, reasonable risk taking, a solid sense of self, and tenacity are always valuable traits, but the only trait absolutely required is *desire,* you must want to own your own business.

ACTION STEP 3   *Take the "Entrepreneurial Quiz"*

The best way to start exploring the entrepreneurial ownership option is to answer three questions:

Can I run it?

Will I like it?

Should I do it?

"Can I run it?" This is simply a matter of whether you have the knowledge and skills to make the business a success. The process of analyzing your knowledge and skills will be covered in Part 3. Your task here will be to determine what knowledge and skills the business requires.

It's important that you do a fairly detailed analysis. The business requirement and your background may both include financial management, for example. Your financial management experience may be compiling and analyzing financial information, but the business may require someone who knows how to keep its banker happy when cash gets short.

Sales management to you may mean conducting research, setting annual goals, building a national plan, and implementing a sales compensation program. To the small company, sales management may mean personally accompanying the salespeople on calls to learn what the market wants and the salespeople need. In a small company, you may be the sales force.

The same care needs to be taken with manufacturing—you may be able to devise productivity programs, whereas the business needs a practicing engineer.

These examples have two interesting dimensions. First, most corporate managers are experienced in only one or a few disciplines. Business ownership usually requires broader expertise in all basic disciplines.

Second, corporate managers experienced enough to be thinking about their own business are probably senior enough that they have for some time been able to delegate detailed tasks. Tasks like approving customer credit and devising equitable weekend work schedules may be important in a small business and the owner-manager will be required to do them.

The point is, you need to understand in detail what it's really going to take to run the business.

Of course, someone doesn't have to have all the knowledge and skills the business requires. You can learn them or hire someone for them, but you should be mindful that you might incur higher cost and might become dependent on someone else.

"Will I like it?" This question relates to the obvious fact that there are more considerations to business ownership than having the competence to run it. Enjoyment and satisfaction are going to come more from other things. Here is a list of some additional criteria to explore that may have a bearing on whether or not you'll like having your own business:

- How much money you need to earn
- How much money you want to earn
- Location
- Risk
- Liquidity
- Growth potential
- Competition
- Physical working conditions
- Status and image
- People intensity

While any or all of these may be especially important to you, the last three deserve some special attention.

At first glance, *physical working conditions* may seem trivial inconveniences and a small price to pay to have your own business. But after the initial excitement wears off you may think differently. A small inelegant open office may be tolerable at first, but its lack of privacy may wear on you. True economy travel is even more vexatious than the standard corporate variety. And everyone talks about the hours of the typical business owner. ("I only work half a day— from 7 a.m. to 7 p.m.") The pace may be exhilarating for a few weeks, or even months, but it can become overwhelming.

Status and image, whether we like it or not, do depend to some degree on what we do for a living. In some cases corporate employment actually provides the symbols of status such as club membership, limousine service, social visibility, and so on. Business ownership provides its own status, but it is not as widely recognized as the status of senior corporate employment.

People intensity is the easiest of these criteria to underestimate. In some parts of the country and in some businesses, hiring people requires enormous effort. Even if hiring isn't a problem, managing people in a small business takes more time and face-to-face communication, and even confrontation, than the corporate person may be used to. The management of people can become so time-consuming that it can seem to be "in the way" of running the business. Of course, it *is* the business.

"Should I do it?" The third question examines aspects of business ownership which are inescapable no matter what the business.

Loneliness is one. There may be many things wrong with corporations and corporate employment, but they can provide support— both psychological and physical. The infrastructure of a corporation usually provides employees with plenty of feedback and reinforcement. Not so for the entrepreneur. The loneliness of ownership can sometimes play tricks on the imagination and magnify successes and failures out of proportion. A strong sense of self and personal confidence are needed to handle the loneliness.

Pervasiveness is a less-recognized aspect of business ownership. Stated simply, your business can come to affect every part of your life. Employment may let you compartmentalize life and keep your job separate from your personal and family matters. However, the time and emotional demands of business ownership can invade any safe haven a person might have. The responsibilities are present 24 hours a day.

Risk is the best known of these universal considerations. Even though corporate employment has become more risky, business ownership still represents a higher and more total risk. Failure as a business owner can result in a loss of wealth and savings, self-esteem, business reputation, and personal happiness. The losses may even strip away the resources needed for future opportunities.

Although these general considerations have been presented last, they should be examined first. They apply to *all* business ownership.

ACTION STEP 4 *Learn the Four Routes to Ownership*

If you are considering going it on your own, here are your four options and how they compare in terms of advantages and disadvantages. You can:

1. Start a business.

2. Form a professional or consulting practice.

3. Own a franchise.

4. Buy an established business.

The preceding list begins with the highest-risk but normally lowest-cost route—starting a business—and ends with the lowest-risk but normally highest-cost route of buying an established business.

ACTION STEP 5   *Examine in Detail How to Start a Business*

Starting a business may, under some circumstances, be a better alternative than buying one. It can be cheaper, faster, and less complicated. It can result in a business which matches the owner's criteria exactly.

Some are easy to start. Some businesses, particularly service businesses, are easy to start. Real estate sales companies, repair services, small restaurants, and professional service practices (accounting, legal, financial, medical) can all be started without great difficulty. They may take time to grow and the entrepreneur still may come out ahead by buying, but starting some businesses is easy.

Some should be started. If someone has a unique idea or some special personal advantage, the alternative of starting a business should be examined. A special personal advantage might be a patent, a location, or a ready-made client/customer base. A person may have a one-of-a-kind source of supply, a unique talent, or some special relationships that will ostensibly ensure success.

Sometimes it's the only way. When the desired business isn't available or affordable, starting one is the only way. In the case of a unique idea—a new product or service, say—you may have no alternative because there are no such existing companies.

But the risk is higher. "*Seven* out of every *ten* new businesses fail within the first five years." This often-quoted statistic shouldn't surprise you. A business which has survived five years has proven that its products, prices, location, and its methods of operation are acceptable to its market. These key components in the start-up business are all unproven.

Under-capitalization and lack of required skills are the two major reasons for new business failure. Both are the result of the high uncertainty in business start-ups. A profitable, cash-generating, existing business may cost a premium to buy, but it may be worth it.

The Process. Starting a business requires three things: a marketable idea, a plan, and the resources to carry out the plan.*

The Idea. The idea for the new business need not be a new idea, your idea, or even a good idea, but it does have to be a *marketable* idea. Here are some questions to pose:

- Does the idea address a real need or want? Is there, or could there be, a demand?
- Will the demand be big enough to support a business? Is the field open or crowded with competition?
- Can the idea actually be transformed into a business? Is the technology available? Will the cost result in a product or service at a price the market can or will pay?
- Do you have the knowledge and skills required? Has anyone else tried this idea? What was the outcome and why?

Answering these questions takes much thought, a lot of research and, very often, some intuition.

The Plan. The plan for a new business will be a paradox. It is based on projections and conjecture. There is no historic pattern or experience base to use as a guide. Yet, unless the business is simply a hobby, the new business plan is expected to be exceedingly detailed. Here is a plan outline:

1. *General concept statement.* The business idea may not be obvious to anyone but you. If others are expected to be financial or human resources, the plan will need to provide them with a succinct description. The concept statement should describe the idea and summarize its potential risks and rewards.

2. *The product or service.* The description of the product or service will include costs for varying levels of production, the name and

---

* Of course, if the entrepreneur has customers waiting to buy the new product or service, then we know the idea is marketable and can certainly develop a plan. Anyone with customer orders can usually get the resources needed.

the packaging if there are any, and any uniqueness or competitive advantage. The plan should describe any protection for the product or service and the barriers others would face upon entering the field.

3. *The market.*   The market can be defined in several ways:

Size

Composition/segments

Growth

Profitability

Location

Competition

Demographics

The typical plan describes how the buying decision for the product or service is made and who makes it. It presents the pricing rationale and describes the competitive environment. It explains any special features about the market, such as distribution methods, cyclicality, government impact, and so on.

4. *The schedule of events.*   A key to a start-up plan is a detailed schedule of all the events involved in bringing the new business on-stream. The schedule should show *what* the event is, *when* it occurs, including, if it's appropriate, when it begins and ends, and *who* is responsible for each event. No list could be complete, but here is a sample of the kinds of events to schedule:

- Completing the design of the product or service and its packaging
- Selecting suppliers
- Hiring employees
- Choosing a location
- Developing brochures
- Creating advertising and promotion programs
- Obtaining licenses and permits
- Setting up special announcement meetings
- Scheduling customer contacts
- Setting up shop—furniture, telephones, tools, computers, supplies, etc.

- Selecting distributors
- Establishing controls and measurement checkpoints

5. *The budget.* The new business budget must address two special concerns: cash flow and early warnings of trouble. A good format breaks down detail monthly to give a close look at these two key concerns. Owners should learn quickly what weekly or daily indicators can give even earlier warnings.

The Resources. The resources to help start a business include financial resources, physical resources, and information and advice. These resources are not always easy to find or convenient to use. People starting businesses need to be downright ingenious in recognizing and utilizing everything that can help in the extraordinarily difficult task of starting a business.

The new owner's time is the single most important resource in the business start-up. Nothing happens in the start-up of a business unless the owner makes it happen. There are no employees to give help, no long-standing bankers, vendors and suppliers to provide support, and no established customers to offer encouragement.

The owner has to create and build the enthusiasm that will attract others to the idea and to the business. In the beginning, only the owner will have a vision and only he or she will have a stake in its success.

ACTION STEP 6   *Explore Consulting*

Much of the foregoing information on starting a business applies to forming a consulting practice. The major difference is that forming a consulting practice has an added focus on the individual and his or her skills.

Functions of Consultants. The word *consultant* means different things to different people. That's because there are a variety of functions consultants can fill and there are many types of consultants available to do so.

The functions of consulting can include:

- Training
- Problem identification assessment

- Advice
- Problem solving
- Program development
- Special tasks

Any of these consulting functions arise out of needs. The needs have sparked the entrepreneurial consulting profession to respond with services—and products—to fill those needs. Some offer only advice. Others, like certain of the computer consultants, offer products and systems as well.

One generally accepted definition of consulting has these components:

The consultant is from outside the organization.

The consultant has special expertise.

The relationship with the consultant is prescribed by either task or time.

Be aware that while consultants are hired ostensibly to solve problems that either lower costs or increase revenue, there are often subtle nuances to those needs. Figure 2-1 examines some of these subtleties. You have a better chance of staying in demand if you understand them.

To increase sales	To protect a reputation
To save money	To avoid criticism
To save time	To avoid trouble
To save effort	To profit from opportunities
To feel good	To gain control over his or her life
To be popular	To solve a problem
To win praise	To be safe and secure
To gain recognition	To please someone important
To conserve possessions	To end confrontation or sales pressure
To increase well-being	To be different
To be in style	To obey the law
To copy others	

Figure 2-1. Reasons for a consulting engagement.

Models of Consulting Practices. There is more than one way to establish a consulting practice. Figure 2-2 shows five dimensions of consulting, each of which has its extremes.

The first dimension is *degree of effort*. This dimension relates to how much time the consultant plans to put into the consulting practice. The extremes here are fairly obvious: part-time to full-time.

Another dimension has to do with whether the practitioner will do consulting *alone or in association with others*. Consulting firms range from solo practices to huge groups like McKinsey. Some find the small partnerships between these two extremes to be desirable.

The next dimension relates to the consultant's *market strategy*.

The issue here is the market the consultant plans to serve. The extremes range from serving anyone who will buy to serving just one client.

The middle range here is to segment a market according to some criteria of the consultant's ability to serve and the segment's projected profitability.

Another dimension is the *breadth of offerings*. The extremes here range from offering assessment and advice only to offering products, services, newsletters, seminars, and more. The consultant's offerings may change with experience and with market demand.

The final dimension of consulting practices has to do with *how fees are set*. The extremes here are the per-hour or per-diem basis and the retainer basis.

A middle ground variation is the per-project fee. Retainers may be for a period of time to be worked (say, three days each month) or for a specific task to be done (say, handling all export orders each month).

Models of Consulting Practices

1. Degree of effort:	Part-time	Full-time
2. Association:	Solo	Group practice
3. Market strategy:	Any/all	One client
4. Breadth of offering:	Advice only	Products, newsletters
5. Fee basis:	Per diem	Retainer

Figure 2-2. Models of consulting practices.

A special variation is the performance or commission basis where the fee, or a portion of it, will vary with some measure (i.e., savings, people hired, orders received, etc.).

The Positives and Negatives of Consulting. Offering one's knowledge and skills for sale as a consultant is very different from steady corporate employment. This difference brings with it some positives and negatives.

Positives

Freedom.   You choose your work and your working environment.

Earning potential.   If you're good, you can earn large fees.

A way to another job.   A consulting assignment can be a job audition.

Inexpensive to start.   You need no factory, equipment, or inventory.

Flexibility.   You can set your own schedule.

Uses knowledge, skills, contacts.   You are creating demand for your own resources.

Negatives

Lonely.   As a start-up, you have no staff or co-workers to share burdens or experiences.

May provide income, but won't build wealth.   Consulting practices, like most service businesses, do not accumulate assets.

Flow of business is erratic.   Until you are in very high demand, you cannot exert much influence on your clients' schedule of needs.

May involve excessive travel.   If you serve many clients, they will most likely be geographically dispersed.

Requires special skills.   As you will see subsequently, your professional skills are not sufficient to be successful as a consultant. You need more, particularly selling and consulting skills.

Kinds of Skills and Knowledge Involved.   If consulting were just plying expertise for money, it would be a relatively simple task. Consulting requires not only the professional or technical skills the consultant plans to offer to clients, but other kinds of skills as well.

Four kinds of skills and knowledge are:

- Professional or technical
- Business
- Interpersonal
- Consulting

The professional or technical skills and knowledge are those which the consultant plans to offer for sale; the skills which will solve problems, save money, or increase revenue. Here are some examples:

- Human resources skills are used to counter a unionization drive.
- Engineering skills are used to streamline operations and lower costs.
- Sales management skills are used to revitalize a sales force and boost sales.

Now let's consider the *business skills* required. A consulting practice will be a business and, as such, will require skills to manage it. Here are some of the business skills required to manage a consulting practice:

Bookkeeping. This is a business and you must keep records.

Pricing and fee setting. Whether you use competitive pricing, incentives, cost-plus, or just charge what the market will bear, you need the skills to set prices.

Negotiating. Clients bargain for consulting services. You need the skills to win.

Marketing. From segmenting the market to pinpointing needs and trends, these skills are essential.

Selling. The key skill for a personal services business is the skill of personal selling.

Promotion. Potential clients need to know who you are, what you do, and how to engage you.

Strategic and tactical planning. The real challenge is often not so much what you *will* do, but you *won't* do. As a solo practitioner you need the skill to plan your time.

Goal setting. Activity can feel satisfying to the new consultant, but goal achievement is what's needed.

Research. There is a set of skills involved in digging out facts, locating resources, uncovering new techniques, and analyzing markets. Research can hold the key to understanding demand.

Consulting requires a fairly solid base of *interpersonal skills.* Consultants have no authority to direct change, yet they are expected to be the agents for change. Consulting often takes place in emotionally charged, troubled organizations. Here, then, are some of the interpersonal skills required of a consultant.

Listening. Consulting success depends on understanding the client, and the best skill to gain understanding is listening.

Diplomacy. The skill to blend honesty with tact is not common in all of us.

Communications. You will not be in the client's organization as a full-time person, so your ability to hear and be heard will require extra skill.

Gaining trust. If the organization mistrusts you as an outsider, or for any reason, you cannot do a good job.

Persuasiveness. To be effective you will need to influence people even though you do not have authority over them, and that takes the skill of persuasion.

Conflict resolution. Consultants are usually called into problem situations, and that often means that conflicts surround the potential solutions.

Group dynamics. Any recommendation you might make has to consider how individuals work in groups and how groups work together.

Meeting skills. Almost all of your contact at the client company will be in the form of meetings. Gatekeeping, summarizing, brainstorming, and idea testing are examples of the skills involved in handling meetings.

Overcoming fears. Your effectiveness will be diminished if people in the client's company are afraid of you. You need the skill to recognize and dispel their fears.

Setting realistic expectations. Though self-explanatory, the skill to set and continually manage expectations may be second in importance only to selling skills for the consultant.

Because consulting is an activity of its own, it has its own requirements for *knowledge and skill about consulting.* The key requirements are:

Contracting. The contract terms of a consulting engagement spell out what both parties want. Your knowledge and skill in structuring the contract can make the difference between a rewarding assignment and one that is a financial or professional disaster.

Diagnosis. Your ability to diagnose the client's problems is the output of your listening and research skills and forms the cornerstone of your approach to the assignment.

Developing recommendations. Recommended solutions need to be both valid and practical. A dissertation which merely states some astounding insight into the client's problem isn't a solution. Neither is a brilliant solution which can't be implemented.

Reporting. Keeping the client informed avoids surprises and acts as a quality-assurance procedure.

Presentations. Your sales pitch, your contract proposal, your reports, and your recommendations are all likely to require the skills to make a presentation.

Working with the organization. It takes skill to understand and work with the political and informal power structures of an organization, particularly when you are an outsider and a possible threat.

Supporting the sponsor. Not infrequently, the consultant's sponsor is a part of the problem. It takes skill to provide the support to stay engaged and still not sacrifice the impartiality that the solution demands.

Experienced, professional consultants worry that the newcomers with only corporate experience lack the appreciation for these special consulting skills.

The Importance of Marketing and Selling. The biggest surprise for most beginning consultants, and by far the biggest reason for the

failure of consulting practices, is the difficulty of marketing and selling consulting services.

A consulting practice differs from some other kinds of businesses
because of the way business is generated.

Little repeat business.   Most consultants do only one job for a
client. If the problem is solved, there is no repeat business, though
there may be an opportunity for different assignments.

No way to forecast.   There are neither specific data nor valid tools
for an individual to do detailed forecasting.

Many peaks and valleys.   While it's difficult do forecasting, large
trends affecting your market and your clients will lead to coinci-
dental surges and plunges in demand.

Hard to influence demand.   While you can do a lot to let clients
and potential clients know about your services, you can do little to
truly affect their need for them.

Concepts of market power and market share don't apply.   The
economies of scale and the benefits of the learning curve that
typically come from growth aren't really applicable to a personal
service business. The largest share you can have is one person's
worth.

These differences imply a need to generate business constantly and
to build on every opportunity.

There are other reasons why consultants need to promote and
build.

- The needs of past clients change. Sometimes when a consultant
  solves a problem, he or she has effectively erased any chance of
  further employment with that client.

- Contacts change. More than with product sales, consulting is
  bought on the basis of personal contacts and relationships.
  Because people at the client company change jobs and companies, even a long-successful consulting practice can find itself with
  no business when it loses its personal contact at its largest client.

Developing and building a consulting practice has been called a
numbers game. If it takes five presentations to get one contract and
twenty contacts to get one presentation, then it takes one hundred

contacts for each contract. Imagine a funnel which needs constant refilling.

All of this reinforces the idea that consulting practices are less like farming and more like fishing. In farming you plant a crop, tend it, and it grows, the same way most businesses work. With fishing, you have to work at it all the time and there is no natural growth. In farming, if the soil is weak you can fertilize. In fishing, if there aren't any fish, you have to move to another place.

A rule of thumb says that approximately *50 percent* of a beginning consultant's time should be spent marketing and selling. That means only half the consultant's time is available to bill and earn money.

That also means the consultant has to have fairly well-developed selling skills and the willingness to engage heavily in the selling function. It bears repeating that *the biggest reason for failure in consulting is lack of effective marketing and sales.*

ACTION STEP 7 *Check Out Franchises*

One increasingly popular way to stay in demand is to learn how to own and operate franchises. Franchises are often called *turnkey entrepreneurship* and, as such, they offer some special appeals, particularly to the first time business owner. Most come with tested systems to help manage the business. From the sign over the front door to the payroll accounting system, the franchisee has the franchisor's experience and support available. Many established franchisors have field consultants who visit the locations on a regular basis and when called to help with problems.

A common expression used to describe owning a franchise is: "Be in business for yourself but not by yourself." Owning a strong franchise can make the buyer instantly a part of a large organization with sophisticated advertising and strong market recognition.

Buying a franchise is a fairly straightforward proposition. Federal and state laws require the franchisor to disclose the material facts about the franchise and its offer to sell. There is little negotiating. This is considerably different from buying an established, nonfranchise business where financial data may be vague and the price is determined only after lengthy negotiations.

The franchise industry enjoys a better reputation than in years past. The super successes in the field, such as McDonald's, coupled with tight government regulation and policing by the industry itself, have raised the image of franchises. While there are still bad franchises and dishonorable franchisors, there is generally a more positive view toward franchise ownership.

Franchises are now available in a much wider variety and price range. One recent collection of franchise offerings contained a $3000 franchise to provide business education seminars and a $1 million top-name restaurant franchise. In between were franchises for instant printing ($35,000), hair styling ($75,000), automotive repair ($100,000), and even a basketball franchise ($250,000).

This variety means people have more chances to find opportunities which match their desires and their financial capabilities, making franchises attractive and affordable to more people who are seeking to become entrepreneurs.

What Is a Franchise?   A franchise is a license. In most cases, it is a license to use a franchisor's name and to offer its products or services for sale in exchange for certain fees. The terms of the license are spelled out in a franchise agreement.

The Franchise Agreement.   This agreement will cover in detail the obligations the franchisee (buyer) and the franchisor have to each other. It will include:

- The price of the franchise, the terms of any financing, and the ongoing royalty schedule.

- A list of exactly what the franchisee is getting for the money. In addition to the right to use the franchisor's name and to sell the products or services, the franchisee may be getting training, certain equipment, a starting inventory, special promotions, or a number of other things.

- The procedures which must be followed in operating the franchise. Some franchises have very detailed manuals that cover all aspects of operations, from what color uniforms are required to how to clean the floors. Some franchises permit a degree of flexibility; others require strict adherence to procedures. All require some form of reporting and controls.

- The duration of the agreement and the procedures governing sale, renewal, and transfer. Also covered are the conditions under which either side may cancel the agreement.

- A definition of the territory. The territory may be narrow or broad, exclusive or unprotected, or some combination which might even change over time.

- A definition of the responsibilities for operations. The agreement covers the responsibility for pricing, purchasing, advertising, paying invoices, hiring, training, insurance coverage, maintenance, security and similar items. Some franchisors require the franchisee to operate their franchise personally. If the franchisor provides consulting or troubleshooting support, it should be covered in the agreement.

- The plan for the facility. Some franchisors provide the complete facility, others give detailed specifications, and others offer little or no guidance. Some franchisors own the facility and lease it to the franchisee. In other cases, the facility is rented from a landlord— sometimes from the franchisee.

The franchise agreement is an imposing and important document which the franchisee's attorney should review.

The Up Side of Owning a Franchise. The most obvious benefit provided by a franchise is an established, tested product or service. Equally important can be the methods and systems which have been refined to a smooth set of procedures and which have been proven successful. Franchisees are able to benefit from the franchisor's learning curve.

The strong franchisor is almost certainly able to secure a better location than an individual. The franchisor has more technical expertise in site selection and has more financial clout to negotiate and sign up good locations.

If the franchisor is a heavy advertiser and promoter, the recognition factor can be a big plus for the franchisee. The economy of scale available to the franchisor can permit advertising on television and other media too expensive for the independent operator.

Economies of scale may extend to purchasing of materials and supplies, giving the franchisees lower prices than they could obtain on their own.

Training, consulting, and any other kinds of help the franchisor provides can be very meaningful. The independent operator has limited and often expensive resources for help. The buyer may appreciate the availability of the franchisor's field staff.

The Down Side of Owning a Franchise.   The *restrictions and controls* imposed by the franchisor are one drawback to a franchised business. The franchisor may be able to enforce rules and procedures regarding cleanliness, dress, colors, hours, and much more.

Franchisees may be prohibited from expanding or relocating their business because of the franchisor's licensing of others. If the franchisor requires franchisees to purchase its products and supplies and does not permit them to buy on the open market, they may pay uncompetitive prices.

The *license fee and ongoing royalties* can seem onerous, particularly if franchisor support is weak.

The ownership of the franchise license is not permanent. This could pose a serious problem later, especially if the owner wants to sell or bequeath the business. The franchisor's management and financial strength may become weak or may fail. Franchisees can be adversely affected by events outside their control.

Finding the business is actually a little easier with a franchise. If buyers know which franchise they want, they can make contact directly. If not, here are some easily available resources to help you in the decision:

Franchise Opportunities Handbook
Superintendent of Documents
U.S. Government Printing Office
Washington, DC 20402

Membership Directory (and other publications)
International Franchise Association
Suite 1005
1025 Connecticut Ave. NW
Washington, DC 20036

Directory of Franchising Organizations
Pilot Books
347 Fifth Avenue
New York, NY 10016

The Disclosure Document.   Franchisors are required to publish a disclosure document that will give buyers more information than they can ever hope to get from an independent business owner. The document covers:

- The description of the franchise
- The franchisor's ownership and financial condition
- Background data on key people
- The price, royalties, territory, and other terms of the franchise license (including any financing which may be available)
- The operational duties of the franchisee
- Any other obligations of the franchisor, such as training, advertising, and promotion
- The procedures for sale, repurchase, default, termination, renewal, and transfer of the franchise
- The procedure to establish the physical location
- Any litigation in which the franchisor is or has been involved
- Any restrictions on purchases or sales by the franchisee
- Information about past, present, and projected franchise locations including, where appropriate, the names of the franchisees

Other Franchisees.   The last item on the foregoing list can help buyers locate other franchisees. Buyers can get valuable insights into the franchisor's behavior and performance by talking with people who have had firsthand experience. Buyers can find out if promises were kept and how the quality of the goods, services, training, and other support compared to what was expected.

By locating the former owners of failed locations, buyers may be able to get some very useful, although possibly tainted, insights into the downside risks of the franchise.

The Franchisor.   Of course, the franchisor itself is the prime source of information. The buyer may be subjected to a high pressure sales approach or may have to initiate the contact, but either way, there is plenty of information available.

The franchisor will want information about the buyer, too. References, a summary of experience, and a financial statement are a minimum. The buyer may also be asked to prepare a business plan to demonstrate his or her ability to manage the franchise. See p. 27 for an outline of a basic business plan.

Judgment Required.   The real job in buying a franchise is to exercise good judgment on all the information available.

- Is the franchise a good value? What do buyers get that they couldn't provide for themselves or obtain by buying a nonfranchise for the same price?

- Is the franchisor reputable and financially stable? Are the people competent and trustworthy?

- Are the financial projections realistic and achievable? The key element in the projections is the market potential.

- Does this franchise satisfy the your basic criteria: Will you like it and can you run it?

ACTION STEP 8   *Consider Buying an Established Business*

This alternative appears complicated but it really involves just six straightforward steps.

1. Prepare While You're Still Employed.   Line up your accountant, attorney, and other advisors. Have them show you how to lock in any severance benefits you might have, and how to get set up. Line up the insurance you will need. Get business cards and stationery. Provide for whatever secretarial services you might want. A low-cost way is to buy an inexpensive answering machine and use a secretarial service as needed. Work out of your home if you can. (Figure 2-3 describes some benefits of working from home.) If you know what kind of business you want, learn as much as you can about it now. If you can, spend time in the market and with customers to find out what's important to them.

Consulting and service businesses can be started and run from home. Figure 4-1 lists 25 of them. Here are some benefits to doing so:

1. You keep costs low at a time when it's most important to do so.

2. In addition to the tax advantages of whatever business you have, you can deduct certain household costs as office expenses.

Figure 2-3. Benefits of working from home.

2. Decide on What Kind of Business You Want. Here is where the questions "Can I run it?" and "Will I like it?" are important. You will have taken a personal inventory of your skills and knowledge, and thought about what you want for location, risk, growth potential, working conditions, and, of course, income.

To get an idea of the kinds of businesses that are out there look in the "Business Opportunity" classified section of your newspaper. Visit a variety of businesses to see what owning one of them might be like. Unless you are going to be a direct competitor, most business owners will be helpful in telling you what ownership really involves.

3. Determine What You Can Afford. Start with how much you have and how much you can borrow. Then add how much you can *save* by cutting back your expenses. Develop a detailed personal budget showing what you absolutely need to get by.

Keep in mind that business sellers usually allow buyers to pay part of the price as a down payment and then pay the balance over several years, much like a mortgage.

4. Find the Business. Reading "Business Opportunity" ads and working with business brokers are both good, but passive, steps. To find exactly what you want, you may need to conduct an active search. This involves using direct mail, telephone, and personal networking to contact directly the owners of businesses you are interested in buying. Remember to examine the wide variety of franchises.

5. Analyze the Business. Your own common sense applied to some basic questions and answers will do wonders. Business analysis is a well-known process. Your accountant and attorney will help.

How much to pay is always a key question. Begin with establishing the value of the business, what it's worth.* Use three keys to value the business:

- What it *owns*—the market value of its assets

- What it *earns*—its real cash flow

- What makes it *different*—an assessment of its risk

Once you decide what the business is worth—the value—you can decide what you want to pay for it—the price. Price depends on sev-

---

* For a full explanation of valuing and pricing businesses, see *How to Leave Your Job and Buy a Business of Your Own*, by C. D. Peterson, McGraw-Hill, 1990.

eral factors, such as the terms of sale and the relative negotiating skills of the parties.

6. Negotiate and Close the Purchase.   At this point you should have a pretty good feel for how much you want the business and what it's worth. Manage your advisers carefully through this last step. Prepare a checklist of everything that needs to be done and who is responsible for it.

Here is a checklist I use:

- Conduct of the business until closing
- The time and place of closing
- A list of everyone who needs to attend
- A list of all the documents required
- A breakdown of the funds to be disbursed
- Absolute assurance that the funds are available in the amount and form specified
- New corporate tax and employer identification numbers
- Provision for any licenses to be obtained or transferred
- Prorationing calculations for taxes, wages, utility bills, etc.
- Adjustments for any deposits the seller may have with the landlord, suppliers, or utilities
- Transfer of banking arrangements
- Transfer of keys and alarm codes
- Transfer of any computer codes
- The real estate lease or purchase agreement
- Customer lists
- Transfer of utilities—particularly telephone number
- Any separate contracts establishing seller's obligations to consult or to not compete
- Allocation of the selling price to assets, consulting, noncompete agreement, and goodwill
- Provision for broker's fees
- Clearance of outstanding liens or encumbrances

- Compliance with bulk sales laws to notify suppliers
- Assumption or discharge of any other leases or mortgages
- Definition of the warranties and guarantees the seller will provide
- Provision for security by the buyer
- Definition of the seller's obligations to help in the transition of the business and training of the buyer
- Adjustments for actual inventory and receivables value at closing
- Adjustments in the event that accounts receivable are not collected
- Disposition of any outstanding claims or litigation against or by the seller
- Provision for continuity of insurance or bonding

The entrepreneurial ownership option is not for everyone, but it is one which you should know about and be able to assess.*

---

* For a detailed examination of this option see *How to Leave Your Job and Buy a Business of Your Own* by C. D. Peterson, McGraw-Hill, 1990.

3

Consider Your Conventional Employment Options

The greatest number of options for most people exist in the world of conventional employment; working full time for monetary compensation. You have options within your present company and outside, in other firms.

ACTION STEP 9 *Examine "In-placement"— Reemployment within Your Present Company*

If you are employed, you have a number of conventional employment options within your own company.

Substep 9.1 *Stay Where You Are*

Perhaps because it's so obvious, this is probably one of the most overlooked options. Yet the decision to hold your ground and concentrate on creating a more satisfying situation, or removing the barriers to your happiness, is perfectly legitimate. We will see in Chapter 7 that staying where you are doesn't mean you can tune out, sit back, and relax. This option needn't mean boredom, stress, or unhappiness either.

It does mean that people often have an option in their present jobs to find and build a higher degree of satisfaction. Four factors affect job satisfaction, and you can address each of them in an effort to improve your situation.

1. *Job content.* If your job is too dull or too varied, too demanding or too simple, or if it is unsatisfactory in any aspect of its content, you can feel stressed and pressured. A rational employer will make an effort to construct the content of your job to better suit you because it's in both your interests to do so. Initiative on your part to make well-defined suggestions will make it easier for you to get the changes considered. Consider submitting a revised (or new) job description to your boss.

2. *Working conditions.* Unsatisfactory working conditions may mean excessive hours or travel, uncomfortable surroundings, insufficient resources to do your job, or any number of things that can range from hazardous materials to unsafe practices. Decide what specific unsatisfactory working conditions can reasonably be modified, and then make the effort with your employer to change them. If safety, health, or other agencies should play a role, involve them. The more constructive your proposals, the more likely they will be adopted. Try to offer alternatives and always recognize the cost implications of your suggestions.

3. *Behavioral problems.* Behavioral or interpersonal issues are common and can exist with co-workers, customers, suppliers, subordinates, the general public, your employer, and, yes, you can be a behavioral problem, too. Behavioral problems are pervasive in all of life and you must deal with them as a part of living. If you haven't acquired the skills to build working relationships, constructively confront problems, and resolve conflicts, get them now. Your company may offer courses in these skills. If not, visit a library, find some seminars, or, if you think your problem is serious, seek professional help.

4. *Compensation.* Pay, benefits, and other elements of compensation are notorious job dissatisfiers. If your employer has any experience, he or she is prepared to deal with your concerns about salary and compensation issues. Get data from your human resources department, other companies, or from outside agencies so that you can be factual and creative in your approach. Here's a tip: Tie your

arguments as closely as you can to your good performance and comparable pay in your industry.

The key to improving your satisfaction in your present job is to confront any of these factors which are causing your discontent. Few people attack these problems head-on, possibly because of some old assumptions about how people have to adapt to work rather than the other way around. More likely today is a fear that complaining malcontents will be high on the list when layoffs are planned or can easily be replaced by a host of eager job seekers. Whatever your problem, solving it can be your simplest and most profitable option.

Substep 9.2   *Consider Promotion, Demotion, and Side-Stepping*

The traditional notions of in-company mobility involve the more or less formal matching of your business skills, knowledge, and performance with your employer's needs, typically as part of your employer's development programs and at your employer's initiative. If they even exist, many such company programs atrophy after a little use and some are failures from the beginning.

Here is another place where you can exercise initiative. By knowing your company thoroughly, you will know where it is growing or contracting. You will know or can find out where it needs new, better or added skills. We will see more in Chapter 7 concerning how to find and reach the people who can affect your in-company mobility.

Base your initiative on more than a conventional look at your job experience and the jobs which those experiences might suggest. Examine all parts of your education and any specialized training you've had. Even your hobbies may give you some special qualifications. Your strong desire and a good work history might convince a hiring manager to give you an opportunity in a different field.

As an example, many companies today have recognized that the weakness of the dollar makes U.S. goods a bargain for foreign buyers. As these companies prepare to enter the export market they will have needs for people with international skills: languages, cultural and political savvy, in-country experience, and similar skills. Having or acquiring these needed skills can become the basis for a career initiative.

Your most powerful initiative will be to develop your skills and knowledge on your own, and to manage your own in-company mobility to ensure that you stay in demand.

Substep 9.3   *Restructure Your Job or Create a New One*

Every company has special problems and opportunities that can go unnoticed and unaddressed for years. Among the most in-demand skills are those that can save your company money or increase its revenue. Either of these is an area ripe for exploration. The first step is to conduct a systematic search for such problems or opportunities. When you isolate a few, decide which ones (be realistic) would be most interesting and rewarding to work on and which would have the biggest payoff for your company. The next step is to train yourself or get the training needed to be a subject-matter expert in those areas.

This tactic is growing in popularity as people become more self-reliant. Once you have the in-demand skills you want (see Part 3) and have analyzed the problems and opportunities in your company, you are in a position to propose a job that matches the two. Be crystal clear when you describe how you can solve those problems (lower costs) or take advantage of those opportunities (increase revenue).

ACTION STEP 10   *Examine "Outplacement"— Employment Options outside Your Present Company*

This is not a job search book. There are many books on all aspects of finding a job. Some job search fundamentals will be covered in Chapter 5, but in this chapter we want to develop and explore employment options that may not have been obvious to you.

Substep 10.1   *Do the Same Job in a Different Setting*

You can do the same thing you're doing now in a variety of different settings:

1. Another company in your industry where your industry knowledge enhances the value of your job skills

2. A larger company where you can grow more professionally in your present skills

3. A smaller company or division where you can broaden and add to your skills

4. A different geographic location where your skills and knowledge might be in higher demand

Substep 10.2   *Take on a Different Job*

As we saw, you can use past experiences, formal training, hobbies, or just plain desire to get a job in a whole new field inside your company. Of course you can do the same thing outside your company as well.

You can use the same strategies to *create a job* in another company that were suggested on p. 50 to create a job inside your company.

Some jobs, such as real estate sales, require little previous special background, as the essential skills and knowledge are usually provided in some way by the hiring firm.

Police, fire, and craft apprenticeship programs in some fields allow for new untrained entrants, though educational and physical qualifications do exist.

Other jobs require few skills at all. Entry-level and unskilled positions exist almost everywhere, though in some places the competition is keen among the unskilled unemployed.

Sometimes brass nerve and a silver tongue can get a person a job for which he or she is not qualified. If that person is a quick study, success is not impossible.

"Celebrity" status can bring job offers to the unqualified. Professional athletes are sometimes given a chance at jobs because the people hiring them believe the athletes can become qualified and that their marketing or other value to the firm is worth the risk and expense of the learning curve. If you have any celebrity status at all, you can leverage it to advantage.

New industries create new jobs and new career opportunities. By definition, the people who first fill these jobs will be unskilled at them.

Labor shortages are uncommon now, but forecasters predict a big shortage in the future and those shortages may bring a desperation to hiring firms that will force them to hire the unqualified.

4

Consider Some (Slightly Offbeat) Alternative Employment Opportunities

Maybe a full-time, full-pay company job isn't for you. Maybe corporate demand for your knowledge and skills has evaporated. You have alternatives. Part of staying in demand is knowing how to locate special—some might say offbeat—opportunities.

These alternatives might serve as interim or temporary arrangements. They can become long-term arrangements for those who form new expectations. They can keep skills and contacts alive and can add to the demand for your personal enterprise.

These aren't fantasy trips; they are very real alternatives. Some are new. Some are just overlooked. You may not qualify for some and you may not want others, but you should know about all of them. Following are 31 you might want to consider.

ACTION STEP 11 *Remember the Armed Services*

No longer do the armed services accept anyone who breathes. The armed services are cutting back and downsizing just like civilian institutions, and they are carefully controlling their human resources. They are still seeking new enlistees, although perhaps now they are looking for even *fewer* "good men."

ACTION STEP 12 *Understand Bartering*

Singing for your supper may not be an alternative for you, but trading labor or skills for housing, services, or goods is a real possibility. Barter need not be direct. Three-way barter where, for example, your landlord doesn't need your advertising skills but the landscaper does. So you develop a campaign for the landscaper who in turn takes care of the property for the landlord who gives you credit on your rent.

ACTION STEP 13 *Consider Care-Giving*

The elderly, the sick, and the children of working parents need care, and the skills involved in giving care are not all professional skills.

The opportunities are not exclusively in the voluntary sector. Many are paying jobs available to you as an independent contractor, while others are available to you through organizations.

You should know that health care is the fastest growing segment of our economy, as more and more people want more and more services from better and better technology.

ACTION STEP 14 *Work on Contract*

Working through an agency for a company on a specific task under a defined contract is an increasingly popular way for people to work and for companies to keep down their permanent rolls. Once confined to laborers, truckers, or technicians, contracting now enthusiastically embraces white-collar workers. Contract-employment agencies exist for the traditional kinds of contract work, and now some general employment agencies deal in contract labor.

Examples of contract labor today are computer programmers, charter flight crews, and nurses.

An important variation, independent contracting, is covered subsequently.

ACTION STEP 15   *Be a Courier or Chauffeur*

Delivering documents to secret agents abroad isn't much called for now, but some people still want their cars couriered from Miami to New York. And many people want to leave the driving to someone else on occasion.

ACTION STEP 16   *Down-scale*

Scaling back your material goals and your career ambitions can open up many new options for you. Casting off a high-pressure success image can mean less stress and more satisfaction than a fast track that has no checkered flag. Amy Saltzman, in her book *Downshifting,** calls the process "reinventing success on a slower track." The reinvention can include accepting life on the vocational plateau, seeking less demanding (and presumably more available) jobs, or maybe just finding some different company or rural geography where life is richer in ways other than upscale achievement and materialism.

The trade-offs between satisfying material wants and following a dream deserve and receive separate treatment at the end of this chapter.

ACTION STEP 17   *Try Flextime*

The alternative here is simply to negotiate with your employer to create employment hours to suit your overall needs. The total hours may be more or less, but in most cases are the same as a regular job. Flextime is an appealing alternative for people who have responsibilities such as child care, or those who are involved with other activities, or who are in transition to a new way of life.

* *Downshifting,* Amy Saltzman, HarperCollins.

ACTION STEP 18   *Serve in Government or Charities*

Public service as an employment alternative is not the nonpaying volunteer work, but the elected or administrative jobs in local, state, or national government and the administrative jobs in such organizations as the Red Cross.

These paying jobs are still considered public service because people who seek them (claim to) want to accomplish something for the general welfare, and because the pay is usually below that of comparable regular employment.

ACTION STEP 19   *Work in Government*

All levels of government afford employment opportunities, yet private sector people know little about how to research and pursue these jobs.

Research on federal employment opportunities can begin with *The U.S. Government Manual,* which is available in most libraries. If you want your own copy you can write to The U.S. Government Printing Office, Washington, DC 20402. The manual details your contacts for employment in each department of the government. A separate section gives information on employment programs such as those for veterans.

You can buy *Federal Career Opportunities,* which contains listings of available federal jobs and application instructions. The publication can be purchased from Federal Research Services, Box 1059, Vienna, VA 22183. The cost is $38 for three months. State employment can be researched at your state employment office, while local government employment is probably best researched by visiting your city or town hall.

ACTION STEP 20   *Work at Home*

Each week, thousands of Americans decide to work in home-based settings. Some set up home-based businesses. The subject of entrepreneurial alternatives was covered earlier in this chapter, but Figure 4-1 shows 25 in-home businesses which require less than $500 to start.

1. Residential cleaning service
2. Auto detailing
3. Pet sitting
4. Take-out food delivery
5. Word processing service
6. Mail-order business
7. Gift-basket business
8. Carpet cleaning
9. Bed and breakfast
10. Lawn/leaf/snow maintenance
11. Home maintenance worker
12. Home baking service
13. Catering service
14. Computer instruction
15. Consultant
16. Mobile bookkeeping
17. Window washing service
18. Button and badge making
19. Tub and tile reglazing
20. Errand service
21. Novelty balloons
22. Knife sharpening
23. Managing health claims
24. House sitting and management
25. Laundry and tailoring

Figure 4-1. In-home businesses. Source: *Small Business Opportunities,* March 1992.

ACTION STEP 21 *Become an Independent Contractor*

This alternative represents what many see as the biggest trend in employment for the future. As an independent contractor, you are engaged by firms or individuals not as an employee, but as a supplier or vendor who works for a price under a contract for service. One well-known example of independent contracting is the real estate salesperson.

Advantages. Independent contracting offers several advantages to the employer. The independent contractor receives no employee benefits. The employer incurs none of the potential liabilities that go along with the employer-employee relationship, though there are some obligations owed a contractor.

Companies often put projects out for bid with several independent contractors, using the competition among them to get the best deal.

The employer has greater flexibility with an independent contractor. By making limited commitments to independent contractors, the employer can add or remove them from the work force as needed.

This flexibility, combined with the use of competitive bidding and the absence of long-term obligations, makes the use of independent contractors a variable and more easily controlled cost. Companies who have suffered the trauma and cost of downsizing are reluctant to restaff with permanent employees.

From your standpoint, your status as an independent contractor means that you can, in theory, work for any of hundreds of employers, not just one. The opportunities for you to earn money from your skills and knowledge are far broader, and can represent a solid insurance against the vagaries of being tied into one economic unit.

If you have built your in-demand skills as advocated in this book, you will have the ability to select the contract assignments which best suit your criteria for income, content, hours, and other working conditions.

Disadvantages. You do need to know that there are disadvantages to independent contracting. If you have no abilities to market yourself or be marketed by others, you run the risk of not working. Managing your own employment can take a lot of time and work.

In hard times, competition can cause you to work at jobs for less than you might want and work harder to get even those jobs.

A very big difference for you as an independent contractor is that you must provide for your own financial security—medical insurance, disability income, life insurance, and retirement. These coverages can be costly and difficult to obtain. (Financial self-reliance is covered in detail in Chapter 9.)

Minor inconveniences arise from the need to keep records, do billing, and deal with added tax regulations, but for those who want to achieve self-reliance, independent contracting is a well-traveled route.

ACTION STEP 22   *Moonlight*

As the name indicates, moonlighting usually refers to a night job. More specifically, moonlighting is a night or day job in addition to a regular job. Moonlighting can provide added income, added satisfaction, and can be used as a stepping-stone to a change in career.

ACTION STEP 23   *Work Part-Time*

You can take on part-time work as an employee or as an independent contractor. Some of the employer motives of flexibility and cost apply to the increasing acceptance of part-time workers. Workers who have other obligations or who prefer time off make up the bulk of part-time workers, but when full-time jobs are scarce, people will take what's available.

The part-time alternative can mean that you have more than one job for added income, variety, or whatever reasons.

ACTION STEP 24   *Don't Shun Personal Service*

Being a companion, caretaker, cook, maid, or servant for someone may be something you haven't considered. For certain people, this alternative can provide a sense of satisfaction and security not available in any other form of employment.

Personal service can also mean doing those things for more than one person or family. Whatever your view of this alternative, it's one which is very difficult to ignore. Nearly everyone has the necessary skills. Figure 4-2 lists examples of personal service alternatives.

ACTION STEP 25   *Contemplate Religious Service*

It is not extraordinary for someone who has led a secular life to choose to make a change and take up a religious calling. The opportunities are abundant to serve one's religion.

Companion	Guy/gal Friday
Caretaker	House sitter
Cook	Dog walker
Butler	Caddy
Maid	Personal trainer
Gardener	Baby-sitter
Groom	Tutor or teacher
Shopper	Interpreter
Groundskeeper	Masseuse
Home maintenance worker	

Figure 4-2. Personal service jobs.

ACTION STEP 26   *Retire!*

The picture of the elderly retiree quietly living out life's end is not today's picture. With good financial planning, proper habits of health and fitness, conscious career strategies, and a bit of luck, retirement is not an ending, but rather a transition event from being in demand in one setting to being in demand in another. As such, retirement is an alternative.

Retirement wasn't a true alternative in years past. The company pretty much decided what the policies were, and when the employee conformed, he or she was, with few exceptions, retired. Today there are a variety of retirement plans, and policies are as varied as employers care to have them. Be sure you know what your retirement alternatives are.

Unfortunately, just because you are entitled to retirement from one or more companies doesn't mean you will receive any benefits. Some plans, companies, and even insurers have gone broke, leaving pensioners out in the cold. Chapter 9 covers ways to evaluate the soundness of your retirement benefits.

ACTION STEP 27   *Seek Seasonal Employment*

Working in Florida for the winter and in Maine for the summer is a viable alternative if you have the skills that are in demand. Skill at picking citrus fruit and blueberries can give you a Florida–Maine axis, and so can skills in the tourist and hospitality business. With foreign language skills, you might prefer Acapulco and the French Riviera.

Thousands of jobs open up every season somewhere in the world, and possibly right in your part of the world. In colder climes, winter brings ski business, snow clearance, firewood sales, and indoor sun tanning. In warmer spots, agriculture, tourism, and summer recreation offer opportunities.

ACTION STEP 28   *Become a Seminar Leader*

Leading seminars and giving lectures on your own is a business, and may be a high-demand business for you. However, you have an alternative of leading seminars for others. Geneva Corporation (financial services), Fred Pryor (sales training), and The American Management Association (management), are three organizations which engage people to conduct seminars and to lecture on their behalf. Outplacement companies use independent "stringers" to lead training seminars and workshops.

For a thorough treatment of the seminar alternative, see Paul Karasik's *How to Make it Big in the Seminar Business*, McGraw-Hill, 1992.

ACTION STEP 29   *Explore Teaching*

Teaching as an alternative has lots of variations. Public and private education have opportunities from preschool to postgraduate to special and continuing education. Requirements are very stringent for positions involving accreditation or other standards, but are little more than practical and common sense for others.

Your business background may be the full qualification you need to teach an evening course in some aspect of your discipline. If you take required courses in education, you may be able to become fully qualified for broader teaching opportunities, and may open up a rich alternative as a teacher, professor, or education administrator.

ACTION STEP 30   *Try Temporary Work*

The idea of temporary work has changed. "Temping" once meant that a person would work temporarily at a job, often as a fill-in on a permanent job. Today, the jobs are temporary and the person can work full time if he or she chooses and has the in-demand skills. Adia, Kelly, Manpower, and Olsten are agencies specializing in the temporary work alternative.

The ready availability, flexibility, and variety of temporary work make it the first-choice alternative for many people.

ACTION STEP 31   *Volunteer*

Though not a paying alternative, volunteerism does represent a wide range of work and a potential source of great satisfaction. It also represents a potential source of paying employment. A volunteer job can become a paying one if the need can be demonstrated and the funding can be established. Volunteerism is certainly one way to stay in demand.

> Consider Steven and Gwen Lowe. The Lowes have availed themselves of nearly every alternative described in this chapter.
>
> An Army couple, the Lowes took early retirement last year, sold their big house in Washington, D.C. and now live in a sunny upstairs apartment in the home of an elderly couple in St. Petersburg. They pay no room or board; rather, in exchange, Steve does errands for the couple and Gwen takes care of their landlords' medical regimen of pills and shots and does some minor cleaning. They found the couple by advertising in the classifieds.
>
> Steve got some training, became a licensed livery and formed his own company, contracting to work part-time driving people to the airport. Gwen takes frequent temporary teaching assignments. They are active in their church choir.

The Lowe contrivance demonstrates that you can combine just about any and all of the alternatives we have looked at to gain employment, stay in demand, and keep your life rich and full of choices.

The key is going to be your ability to provide yourself with in-demand skills and your willingness to exercise the initiatives to be recognized. Your result will be a lifetime of self-reliance.

PART 3

Reinvent Yourself—Invest in Yourself

A foolish consistency is the hobgoblin of little minds.

Do your work, and you shall reinforce yourself. RALPH WALDO EMERSON
essay on "Self-Reliance"

Your self-reliance depends first on your ability to *produce value competitively*. Whether you work for a company, own your own business, or engage in any of the alternatives discussed in Chapter 2, your efforts must yield something which the market wants and which is of higher value than the market could buy somewhere else.

Your plan for self-reliance has one major complication. You can produce value competitively in many ways, so how do you choose which way to develop and build on? You can follow a conventional approach and adjust your skills and knowledge to changes in the environment as they occur. While this is better than not adjusting, it does put your personal enterprise at risk while you catch up to the changes.

Or, as the economy reinvents itself, you can follow a new approach and reinvent yourself. By consciously examining your own marketability, you can develop a plan aimed at doing what you want to do and being what you want to be.

The process has three parts: learning what the market demands, assessing your personal resources, and integrating your life values. View this process as research and development for your personal enterprise.

5

Reinvent Yourself as Your Own "Personal Enterprise"

If you took your MBA to Wall Street or learned to master robotics on an auto assembly line in Detroit, you know something about demand—it can change.

If you chose to undertake the training and rigors to become a nurse, you know another thing about demand—it can exist even in the worst of times.

If you were a middle-level manager, "coordinating" or "administrating," you know something else about demand—it can vanish completely and permanently.

ACTION STEP 32 *Learn How Employment Value Is Determined by Employers*

Because your self-reliance depends partly on the market's demands, you need ways to analyze where demand is and, more importantly, where it will exist in the future. You can assess demand by industry type, by individual company, by occupation and, most specifically, by type of knowledge and skill.

Demand by Industry Type. One way to assess employment demand is by industry type. It's obvious that growth industries will add jobs, but so will static industries; even declining industries will need new people from time to time.

Growth or decline in an industry may be *cyclical* or *noncyclical* (structural).

Cyclical Industries. The paper industry is a positive example of a cyclical industry. International supply and demand do grow over time, but do so in waves of increases and declines. The U.S. paper industry is competitive on the world scene and continues to invest for the future.

Within the paper industry, segments will grow (paper for copy machines) and others will decline (paper for the old tabulating cards), but for the foreseeable long-term future, with or without recycling, paper is a solid cyclical industry.

In the short run, the paper industry has cutbacks and additions, and it does engage in productivity improvements that eliminate specific occupations. Yet a person with skills that are in high demand by the paper industry has a good foundation on which to build self-reliance.

Less positive examples of cyclical industries are the auto and tire businesses. While supply and demand may grow over the long term, the U.S. industry, with old, high-cost plants, is now in a poor position. Foreign manufactures have made big share gains. Productivity improvements and major cutbacks may continue for some time, making them less desirable places to be unless your skills are those that help make these improvements.

Noncyclical Industries. The structure of demand for some industries does not follow a repetitive cycle but, rather, a life cycle that it goes through once. The nature of the business requires that it constantly develop new products and services as older ones complete their cycle. At the beginning of the cycle, the industry is a growth industry, such as cable television is right now. At the end of the cycle, without the new products or services, the industry declines, much like the hatting industry.

Other Industry Factors. Cyclicality, or the lack of it, is only one factor in assessing industry demand. Here are two more:

Supply and Demand. Some industries, like health care and computers, are facing a demand that seems to have no end. Others, like aerospace and defense looked solid just a few years ago, but now appear to be entering a long period of decline.

Employment Intensity.   Farming produces a growing output with fewer workers, while retail stores hire thousands of people when sales are static. Health care is employee-intensive, while cable television is not. It's not enough for you to pick a growth industry—you need to recognize how that growth translates into jobs.

Your plan for self-reliance can't ignore these important factors, as they can render the value of your skills useless and are mostly beyond your control.

You can learn about industries at any good library. *Business Week* and other magazines publish annual industry roundup editions. Directories like Dun's and others provide facts and rankings. Stockbrokers can analyze and compare industries in many ways.

Demand by Company.   Growth industries will have losing companies, and declining industries will have winners. Your chances of attaining self-reliance depend on your wise choice about which company you work for.

While the chances of an entire industry going from good to bad is rare, it's not rare for individual companies to change from stars to dogs and back again.

During your career, you may decide that a company you are with has become a risk to your self-reliance. The implication of that decision may appear self-centered at first, but it is no different than the decision that a company makes in firing a worker who is not helping its survival. A caring company may try to correct a slumping worker, and you might try to help your slumping company, but self-interest finally dominates.

At some point, you may face a dilemma of choosing your own economic well-being over your loyalty to your firm. The choice is yours, but make it consciously. Don't wait around while Rome burns. Better yet, sniff for smoke regularly. If you get caught by surprise, you may end up buried in a crowd of job seekers unleashed on the market at one time.

You can evaluate companies by talking with employees, suppliers, competitors, and others. If the company is a public one, you can read the annual report and talk with stockbrokers. Business libraries maintain files and directories of articles on thousands of companies.

Most job creation will come from new and smaller companies, and from those exploiting new technology. You can read a study of the 500 fastest-growing small companies published annually by *Inc.* magazine, and a growth study of larger companies done each year by *Forbes* magazine.

Demand by Occupation. There are several studies on future demand by occupation. The most well known is the "Workforce 2000" study done by the Department of Labor. Figure 5-1 from that study shows the 20 professions which are growing the fastest in *percentage* of growth.

Figure 5-2 shows the 20 job categories which will add the greatest *number* of jobs, perhaps 40 percent of the total, between now and the year 2000.

Paralegals
Medical assistants
Home health aids
Radiologic technicians
Data processing equipment
Repairers
Medical record technicians
Medical secretaries
Physical therapists
Surgical technologists
Operations research analysts
Securities and financial
Services sales reps
Travel agents
Computer systems analysts
Physical and corrective therapy assistants
Social welfare service aids
Occupational therapists
Computer programmers
Human services workers
Respiratory therapists
Corrections officers and jailers

Figure 5-1. The twenty fastest-growing occupations (percent growth).

Salespersons, retail
Registered nurses
Janitors and cleaners
Waiters and waitresses
General managers and executives
General office clerks
Secretaries, except legal and medical
Nursing aids and orderlies
Truck drivers
Receptionists and information
Clerks
Cashiers
Guards
Computer programmers
Food counter, fountain, and related workers
Food preparation workers
Licensed practical nurses
Teachers, secondary schools
Computer systems analysts
Accountants and auditors
Teachers, kindergarten and elementary school

Figure 5-2. The twenty fastest-growing occupations (number of jobs).

Some jobs appear on both lists, which means they are adding lots of jobs very fast. Those jobs are *computer systems analysts, computer programmers, food service workers, physical and other therapists, nurses,* and *teachers.*

Demand by Specific Type of Knowledge and Skill. Within those occupations in Figures 5-1 and 5-2 and all the others, lie the specific requirements for skills and knowledge which change with the advent of new methods, new needs, and new technologies.

ACTION STEP 33   *Learn How Demand Changes*

A list of *declining* jobs is shown as Figure 5-3. Like the lists of hot jobs, this list, too, changes.

Tool operator
Inspector, grader, tester
Welder
Vending machine service/repair
Broadcasting technician
Musician
College/university professor
Judge
Petroleum engineer
Government official

Figure 5-3. Ten slowest-growing jobs.

To find out what specific skills and knowledge are in demand today read the help-wanted classified and display ads in the newspapers. *The National Business Employment Weekly* is one good source of the larger display ads which tend to spell out the job requirements more clearly.

Talking with employment agencies and executive recruiters will give you another source of data about today's in-demand skills.

An important source for you is your own company. Your human resources department or others in management should be able to give you ideas about which skills are in demand. Sharpen and use your own powers of observation.

Tomorrow's Knowledge and Skills. Having today's skills and knowledge is fine, but that won't ensure career self-reliance.

The big problem many people face is the obsolescence of their value. Specifically, they don't know enough or can't do as much as the next person to help their company lower costs or increase revenue.

In a poignant "My Turn" column in *Newsweek* magazine, a man in his fifties described his recent firing and the personal trauma surrounding the event and its effect on him. At one point, he told readers how he tried to read the help-wanted ads but *couldn't even understand the language of the requirements.* He was bitter toward his company but made no acknowledgment of his responsibility to keep his own skills and knowledge current (at least current enough to grasp the language of an employment ad).

Developing your skills and knowledge will be an ongoing process. A critical data point in your decision making about your development will be *future* requirements. Your judgment about what kinds of skills and knowledge *will be* needed will determine in great measure how successful you will be at achieving self-reliance. You can get help deciding on tomorrow's skills.

Leaders in your field are one source of information about future needs. Leaders are typically the people who recognize and implement new ideas. They are likely to have a vision of the problems and opportunities ahead.

Academics most often do the research and experimentation that shape the future. Knowing what these people are doing and thinking about can give you a special insight into tomorrow's skills and knowledge.

Analysts may not actually describe the skills and knowledge needed, but they do describe the problems and opportunities, and that's what you need to know. If you can see ahead to the problems and opportunities, you can see ahead to what it will take to meet them. Financial analysts, industry analysts, technical, political, and economic analysts may all have keys to the future.

If you have strategic planning analysts in your own company, they should be able to give you a definitive view of the future problems and opportunities your own firm faces. A discussion might reveal a new thrust or emphasis requiring new skills and knowledge. (Don't forget to sniff for smoke about what might be headed for obsolescence.)

Trade and technical associations are good sources of trends and issues. Spot an issue early enough and you may be able to determine the problems and opportunities which will develop. The problems and opportunities point the way to what knowledge and skills will be needed.

ACTION STEP 34 *Start with What You Have— Conduct a Personal Assessment*

Once you understand what the market wants today and will want in the future, you can take the next step in reinventing yourself— conducting a personal appraisal.

Substep 34.1   *Find and Overcome Your Weaknesses; Find and Exploit Your Strengths*

Personal appraisals are more typically called *assessments*. Assessment techniques have been around for decades, and evolved mainly from the fields of industrial psychology and human resources. Assessments use interviews, tests, and other exercises to explore *interests, personality traits, skills,* and *knowledge.*

A body of test data accumulated over the years, along with professional skill, lets assessors draw some correlations between a person's analyzed results in these four areas and the requirements of various occupations. They can suggest from the test results and interviews the kind of work environment and content most likely to be suited to you. Assessors integrate analyses of a person's aptitudes and preferences to produce their reports.

If you haven't done such an assessment recently, you may find it useful to do so. Among the dozens of books which deal with personal assessment are Bolles' *What Color Is Your Parachute?,** his *The Three Boxes of Life,*† and Krannich's *Careering and Re-careering for the 1990's.*‡

What Color Is Your Parachute? contains a section on locating career counselors.

The Elements of Your Personal Appraisal.   Your appraisal of your personal enterprise, like that of any enterprise, involves an inventory of assets and liabilities. Personal assessment uses certain terms (skills, knowledge, traits, and interests) to take inventory— and you should understand them.

Skills are things you can *do*. They are behaviors you acquire by practice and can demonstrate by actions. Figure 5-4 lists examples of skills.

Knowledge is what you *know*. When reason acts on knowledge, we get understanding. You acquire knowledge by observation in its

---

* *"What Color is Your Parachute?,"* by Richard N. Bolles, Ten Speed Press.

† *The Three Boxes of Life and How to Get Out of Them,* Richard N. Bolles, Ten Speed Press.

‡ *"Careering and Re-careering for the 1990's"* by Ronald L. Krannich, Impact Publications.

Acting	Leading
Adapting	Lifting
Administering	Listening
Calculating	Lying
Charming	Managing
Coaching	Negotiating
Conceptualizing	Organizing
Convincing	Perceiving
Creating	Planning
Cutting	Playing
Dancing	Promoting
Designing	Reading
Driving	Running
Estimating	Selling
Fishing	Speaking
Flying	Supervising
Growing	Team building
Influencing	Threatening
Innovating	Translating
Interpreting	Welding
Judging	Writing
Juggling	

Figure 5-4. Typical skills.

broadest sense, and you can demonstrate it by answering questions. Figure 5-5 gives some examples of knowledge.

While this may appear elementary, the difference between knowledge and skill is important. You are probably able to acquire the knowledge you need to achieve self-reliance. You can learn and understand. The same may not be true for your skills. Skills are behaviors you gain through practice, not study. Juggling will serve as an example. You can learn all the knowledge about juggling that exists—how it works, the laws of physics involved, the history of juggling, the names and motions of every trick. However, with all the practice you might devote to juggling, it's possible that you may never acquire the skills to do it properly.

Architecture	Geography	Places
Company	History	Processes
Competition	Language	Products
Computer	Markets	Technology
Customs	Mathematics	Things
Facts	People	Transportation

Figure 5-5. Examples of kinds of knowledge.

This example might help make it clear. *Medical equipment sales* would rank high on the occupational growth charts in Figures 5-1 and 5-2. Health care is a growth field and will need added sales coverage. It's likely you could learn about the equipment, its features and benefits, the market, the territory, the customers, and the competition. You would have little trouble learning how to manage your time and sales-call pattern. But whether or not you could master the skills of selling—the probe, the presentation, overcoming objections, the tentative close, and all the other techniques of the face-to-face sales situation—is an unknown.

Traits are things you are, characteristics or attributes which are hard to change in adulthood. Figure 5-6 lists just a few traits. Behavioral traits such as "creative" or "mature" are hard enough to examine in ourselves, and nearly impossible for others to help us assess, because traits aren't seen. We can't see "self-motivated." We can see only behavior which *we interpret* as reflecting self-motivation.

One widely used test to analyze personality traits is the Myers-Briggs Type Indicator. The test sets up four dimensions of personality and, by combination, reports results in one of 16 "types." Figure 5-7 lists the four dimensions. Using the italicized initials, the results would be reported as, for example, ENFP—someone who was *E*xtroverted, *I*ntuitive, *F*eeling, and *P*erceiving.

Interests, or preferences, can be analyzed using such tests as the Jackson Vocational Interest Survey or the Strong Interest Inventory. Figure 5-8 presents the Strong Interest Inventory classifications.

Interests are often examined as *occupational* (enterprising, artistic, helping, etc.), *basic* (teaching, sales, advising, law, business, etc.), and through *comparisons* which compare your interests to those of

Articulate	Leader
Assertive	Manipulative
Beautiful	Naive
Charismatic	Old
Confident	Patient
Coordinated	Persistent
Creative	Risk taker
Decisive	Short
Disciplined	Shy
Excitable	Sickly
Fast	Strong
Glib	Tall
Honest	Ugly
Imaginative	Withdrawn

Figure 5-6. Traits: characteristics and attributes.

*E*xtraversion versus *I*ntroversion
*S*ensing versus I*n*tuition
*T*hinking versus *F*eeling
*J*udging versus *P*erceiving

Figure 5-7. Myers-Briggs types.

Realistic
Conventional
Enterprising
Investigative
Artistic
Social

Figure 5-8. Strong Interest Inventory classifications.

people in specific jobs, such as librarian, bank manager, language teacher, and so on.

Substep 34.2 *Know the Limitations of Personal Assessment*

Although personal assessment is widely used, it has limitations in relevance and scope.

Relevance. Any assessment is limited because it is a snapshot in time. It does not consider your potential to add skills and knowledge or to develop different interests. It does not recognize that you can initiate changes in yourself.

An assessment is not a final judgment—it's a tool to guide your initiatives for your future development.

Scope. Unless your assessment involves in-depth personal interviews, it will miss critical factors which affect your career development choices. Your capacity for change has already been mentioned. Other factors not considered in the scope of typical assessments relate to financial resources, social connections, talent, and personal matters.

Financial resources, or the lack of them, can have a big influence on your plan for career self-reliance. Buying a ski resort may satisfy all the assessment criteria you established, but without the money to buy it, you will need another career alternative—say, becoming the manager.

If you have the prospect of putting three children through college at one time, or have other large financial obligations, your career plan has to consider ways to meet those responsibilities.

This is not to say that you can't reject those obligations. People with a passion for their goal have left spouses, walked away from debt, told their children to put themselves through college, and so on.

At the other end of the spectrum is the near-retiree who has prepared well financially and, as a result, has few financial constraints when developing a plan for career self-reliance.

Social connections and status can open many career doors. You can build a career plan around your ability to reach board chairpeople for example. The children of actors have a much easier time forging a career in the entertainment business. High visibility in your community may help you to enter politics, real estate, banking, or personal services.

Typical assessments miss the fact that your particular social values may play a big part in your career planning. Your commitment to an issue such as ecology or child abuse may be so strong that it will drive your career plan and development choices.

Talent—natural mental, creative, or artistic ability—can be overlooked in ordinary assessment because it is not a part of standardized testing, yet talent could easily be the most important component of your personal enterprise.

Personal matters outside the scope of many assessment exercises include the impact of childhood events, unresolved conflicts, and similar psychological issues. Other personal considerations may involve your inability to relocate, a medical condition, your desire for leisure, religious beliefs, or even your commitment to health and fitness.

Personal Appraisal—Imperfect but Necessary. Appraising your personal enterprise, no matter how deeply you go, is admittedly an imperfect exercise. Your interests, traits, knowledge, and skills are complex and changing. Nonetheless, your personal enterprise, like any business enterprise, needs to be appraised as a way of determining its present capabilities and its investment needs.

ACTION STEP 35   *Find Your Life Values—Do What You Love*

Contemplate Lifestyle Issues. Unlike other business enterprises, your personal enterprise is based on you, a living human being, which is more than an inventory of assets and liabilities. You have an intellect which acts on both logic and emotion. The power of strong emotion, *passion,* is important as you think about reinventing yourself. Many of us who work with people in transition and with those seeking more self-reliance, have come to recognize the implications of pursuing a passion.

It takes energy, effort, and sacrifice to go to night school, do book research, take a second job, learn a skill, save a nest egg, or do without some of life's pleasures, but that's just what it takes to learn and develop. You can find agreement on that point in self-help books and other motivational programs, which are all based on the premise that strong desire and a clear goal are prerequisites to achieving human potential.

When traits, knowledge, skills, and vocational preferences are marshaled behind a passion, we see people reshape their personal resources, overcome deficiencies, and even reorient their values. Sacrifices become investments as work becomes pleasure.

Substep 35.1   *Zero in on Your Passion*

Finding your passion may take some work. Look for it in those things you do that make you feel good. Think back on jobs or projects that gave you satisfaction. Do you recall ever having been "in a groove" or "high on life"? (Why was that?) Where does your mind take you when it wanders? (Don't you want to spend real time there?)

Career counselors ask their clients to write their autobiography, including the obituary they want for themselves. They have clients confess their "wanna-be" fantasies.

When people first try these exercises and begin their search, they commonly construct barriers to finding their passion. They load their examination with "oughts" and "shoulds," adopting roles and living by standards which they allow others to set for them.

Work toward simplifying your life and toward stripping away those burdens and any others: unhealthy relationships, meaningless time wasters, bad habits. Make room for your passion.

Substep 35.2   *Integrate Your Passion with Your Career Plan*

Integrating your passion into a career plan for self-reliance takes creativity. "I love to fish but I can't make a living at it" seems to dismiss the whole idea, until we think about the Orvis Company and all the other firms that market fishing equipment and services. A love of cooking may not translate directly to a career as a chef. It may, however, lead you to full or part-time involvement in:

Becoming a food critic

Becoming a home economist

Being a butcher

Cafeteria managing

Catering

Designing kitchens

Farming

Food service contracting or subcontracting

Food, supply, or equipment wholesaling to restaurants

Inspecting food or restaurants

Installing kitchens

Joining a cooking club

Manufacturing food products

Manufacturing kitchen utensils

Nutritional consulting

Owning a bakery

Owning a restaurant

Owning a specialty-food store

Owning a luncheon truck

Publishing a newsletter

Raising organic vegetables

Selling specialty foods

Selling appliances

Teaching cooking

Writing cookbooks

You can use your functional business skills—marketing, finance, human resources—not as an owner, but as an employee in a food-, restaurant-, or cooking-related industry.

One more example may help make the point. If you love the outdoors and fresh air you may not see yourself as a farmer, but how about these possibilities?

Building-supply-yard owner

Civil engineer

Construction company owner

Country club manager

Fisher

Forest ranger

Garden center owner

Gardener

Golfer, tennis player, baseball player, etc.

Grounds keeper

Landscape architect

Law enforcement officer

Lifeguard

Lumber worker

Mail carrier

Marina manager

Milk deliveryperson

Pool maintenance person

Resort owner

Road crew boss

Ski instructor

Surveyor

Utility line maintainer

Yard maintenance company owner

Road builder

Substep 35.3 *Conform Your Passion and Practicality*

You will need to subject any company or job opportunity to the same practical tests you used when considering a business of your own. They are repeated here:

How much money you need to earn

How much money you want to earn

Location

Risk

Growth potential

Competition

Physical working conditions

Status and image

People intensity

Passion can overcome barriers, but some of these important criteria are, for the most part, beyond your control.

Substep 35.4   *Get Help Pursuing Your Passion*

There are some excellent books to help you examine and pursue your passion. Two of them deserve mention.

One is *Do What You Love, the Money Will Follow* by Marsha Sinetar.* In her book, Dr. Sinetar provides a series of inspirational pushes to her reader to "discover your right livelihood."

Another is *Work with Passion* by Nancy Anderson.† Ms. Anderson provides you with a series of specific exercises to help you find, and plan how to do, what you love for a living.

ACTION STEP 36   *Set Your Goal*

Your route to self-reliance depends on your destination, your goal. This section has presented four options for business ownership, as well as employment choices in and outside your company, lists of "hot" jobs, and some (possibly offbeat) alternatives.

The chapter also suggested ways to assess your skills, knowledge, and interests so you can conduct an appraisal of the present state of your personal enterprise.

ACTION STEP 37   *Build a Career/Life Plan to Establish Your Earning Power*

Don't choose your goal based solely on your *present* state. Decide first what you want to do and what you want to become. Find your

---

* *Do What You Love, the Money Will Follow,* Dr. Marsha Sinetar, Dell Publishing, New York, 1987.

† *Work with Passion,* Nancy Anderson, Carroll & Graf Publishers, Inc., New York, 1990.

passion. Next, using your appraisal, determine how your skills and knowledge measure up to what you have chosen.

Your challenge is to fill any gap in qualifications with a plan of personal development. This will be the "investment" in your personal enterprise that will be developed in the next chapter.

Only if the qualification gap is vast and full of requirements beyond your known limits should you adjust the goal. Even then, if in doubt, go for it. Albert Einstein was a poor student, Leon Uris failed English, James Earl Jones once stuttered, Woody Allen flunked a film class, and Abe Lincoln lost a dozen elections on his way to the White House.

Why not try for your first choice and adjust later? The joy of pursuing a paramount goal lends resolve to your efforts and strengthens your self-reliance.

6

Self-Invest
to Build Your
Employment
Value

Secretaries once honed their dictation and typing skills, then they mastered word processing. Now, to be in demand, office support staff need the skills to do graphics for presentations, manage complex communications systems, and more. Soon they will be learning the skills to exploit the new CD Interactive technology. If you don't know what CD Interactive technology is, consider your personal enterprise at a competitive risk. (It utilizes a compact disc and special hardware and software to let you interact with data, text, sound, and video.)

Draftsmen once mastered tedious drawing skills. Then they used templates followed years later by the early *XY* plotters. They learned the first crude computer aided design (CAD) only a few years ago, and now they create movable three-dimensional, video-imaged models from databases of design elements. Tomorrow, instead of designing parts and then assemblies, these technicians will create, view from different perspectives, and even operate complete machines that don't yet exist. It's called *simulation/animation*. If you haven't already thought about how to use a video camera to feed images into your computer, you may learn it from your competition.

ACTION STEP 38   *Commit Yourself to Never-ending Education and Training*

These two examples show that it's not enough to *be* in demand, you must anticipate and prepare for changes to *stay* in demand, even in your chosen field. Some professions require continuing education as a matter of course: aviation, real estate, medicine, and accounting, to list a few. To stay in demand, you must treat your personal enterprise as though it, too, requires never-ending education and training.

ACTION STEP 39   *Decide What You Are Now and What You Want Your Employment Value to Be*

You face more of a task than simply keeping your present technical skills up to date, especially if you are planning to change what you do or where you'll do it. And education alone isn't the answer to self-reliance, as many well-educated (and unemployed) managers, airline pilots, and others will tell you. You have choices of *what* investments to make in yourself, *how* to make them, and which investment *strategy* to follow.

Substep 39.1   *Devise a Self-Investment Strategy That Balances Expertise with Flexibility*

Whether you plan to make your investments in yourself by gradually adding to your present skills or by pursuing a full-time program to gain new ones, you need a defined strategy. The two extremes of self-investment strategy are either to become an expert in one field or a generalist in several. A balance between the two will give your personal enterprise its best security.

ACTION STEP 40   *Become an Expert, Totally Focused*

One investment strategy you could follow is to become a world-class expert in some specialty. You would be in demand to those who need what you do. Your personal enterprise would have a competitive advantage and you should command a premium price. Your expert status could spawn other opportunities, such as writing and speaking, and would help you in your efforts at self-promotion. (See Chapter 7.)

However, relying solely on expertise as a strategy is a risk to your personal enterprise. The specialty you have chosen may be subject to the pressures of a small market or to obsolescence. In the small market, the buyers can exert pressure on your value because you have limited opportunities. Obsolescence can overtake even "modern" specialties, such as those connected narrowly with the defense industry.

Change is a constant and overreliance on this strategy can expose you to the vagaries and whims that can accompany change.

ACTION STEP 41 *Become a Generalist, Stay Flexible*

You can adopt a strategy at the other extreme, and add as many skills as you can manage to your personal enterprise. If the skills you chose are in demand, you will be in demand. You will be well positioned to react to changes in your company's environment. Because you understand several functions, you will work better in teams. Your flexibility will enable you to recognize and adapt to new demands and opportunities.

But accumulating a large number of new skills takes time, energy, and other resources. Done to extreme, it's likely that you will not be able to gain proficiency in any of them. While none of your competitors may have as *many* skills, it's a good bet that several of them have *better* skills, and that relegates you to picked-over and less desirable assignments.

ACTION STEP 42 *Achieve Balance between Flexibility and Expertise*

You can reach a balance by using an "inch worm" strategy. Stretch yourself to acquire a new skill, but then gather yourself up and take the time to become competent at it. Another method is to acquire a group of similar skills, say computer fundamentals and basic literacy, at one time, where the learning is mutually reinforcing.

You will always be recycling your skills, adapting them into newly marketable forms. A career was once like a chess game with known moves and rules, but today it's more like a frightening, quick-reflex, video game with unexpected, often random, twists and turns. A mistake can mean the game—your career—is over.

ACTION STEP 43   *Develop Yourself as an Economic Resource; Choose a Mix of Hard and Soft Skills*

Swapping interest rates, operating a backhoe, constructing benefits plans, selling financial products, and doing desktop publishing are examples of *hard skills.*

Working in teams, making timely decisions, and adapting to changes are all *soft skills.*

Your investment in becoming proficient in hard skills makes you better qualified to *increase revenue* or *reduce costs,* which is the marketable value of your personal enterprise. Gaining soft skills makes you able to apply your hard skills and realize that value. Developing these skills together makes you your own economic resource.

Hard Skills.   Certain hard skills and basic knowledge are nearly mandatory if your personal enterprise is to be competitive.

Language Skills.   These are the foundation of all the skills in your personal enterprise. If you have strong language skills, you have a true competitive advantage. The generally poor level of these skills has drawn fire from education, government, and business leaders. Many Americans cannot read well enough to follow written instructions or write well enough to compose a simple paragraph.

You can enhance your personal enterprise by sharpening your English language skills, and you can do even more for yourself by mastering other languages. The formation of a European Economic Community, the reemergence of Eastern Europe, the potential for capitalism in the former Soviet Union, and the surging power of the Pacific Rim economies all present opportunities for those with in-demand skills. Those skills are worth little if they can't be employed because of a language barrier.

Consider for a moment how much larger the market for your services could be if you spoke just one other language.

As might be expected, English language training in Japan is a billion-dollar business.

Mathematics and Science.   These disciplines, the foundations of technology, are also in bad shape in our general population. Critics say that the monetary reward of financial and business careers has been siphoning the best and the brightest of us away from the sciences.

Although scientific breakthroughs still happen in Silicon Valley, Cambridge, and elsewhere, we can look with some embarrassment at the fact that nearly all recent innovations in manufacturing and quality improvement have come from Japan.

Applying quantitative techniques to solve problems is a hard skill in short supply. If you can add skills such as the capability to do statistical analysis or to construct mathematical models to the other skills in your personal enterprise, you will be more in demand. In Chapter 1, we saw the specific example of manufacturing graduates who also had engineering (mathematical) training being able to command up to $90,000 starting salaries.

Investment in your science skills and their application gives you an ability to innovate, to make improvements, to create and, as a result, to be more self-reliant.

Computer-based Competency.   This is more than simply being literate. Every part of every modern enterprise uses computers. This chapter began with examples of how secretarial work and drafting have embraced these skills and have been changed by them. The change is evident in all disciplines.

Manufacturing schedules push the limits of resource utilization and need on-line systems to function. Cash management has become a minute-by-minute activity requiring computerized networks. Hand-held electronic counters take shelf inventories in stores, while consumer purchasing activity is instantly recorded by bar code scanner analysis of every sale.

You and your family are almost certainly in several computer databases. . . . Just check your mailbox.

Here are six computer fundamentals and their primary functions.

1. *Hardware and operating systems* are the black box parts of the computer world. Most people need only a general understanding of

how computers actually do what they do. You usually can accumulate this knowledge with experience.

2. *Word processing* is the electronic version of typing, editing, composing, and revising text. Many brands of software programs offer spell-checking, a thesaurus, graphic composition capabilities, and more.

3. *Spreadsheets* are the basis for most financial and mathematics work. Spreadsheets create electronic boxes by using one set of labels across the top and another set of labels down the side. For example, you might put the 12 months across the top and the elements of a budget down the side, creating boxes of budget elements for each month. You can then perform any mathematical function you wish on the data in these boxes. Spreadsheets also handle text to support the presentation of the information.

4. *Databases* are essentially files. These might be customer files, parts lists, or anything similar. Database software programs allow you to manage those files. One common use is with mailing lists. Some software is very powerful and has elements of word processing and computation.

5. *Desktop publishing* software allows you to generate wide ranges of type styles and sizes, and permits the use of graphics—from simple icons to elaborate, scanned-in pictures, depending on the software program.

6. *Planning and scheduling* programs are focused on time management and are variations of spread sheets.

You can buy software that combines several functions, typically word processing, database management and spreadsheets.

Selling.   This is a hard skill that can give you both singular and added value. The singular value of being able to sell comes from the ability to increase revenue. If you are skilled at convincing customers to pay money for a company's product or service, you have an in-demand skill, no matter how bad the state of the economy.

Coupling selling skills with your primary hard skills can only add value to your personal enterprise.

Many people tend to think of selling as a discrete function performed by full-time salespeople, but many people in a company could have the opportunity to sell if they have the skills. The credit manager with sales skills knows how to satisfy customers even when saying no. The engineer who can sell adds valuable credibility in contacts with technical buyers. Few sales calls are more effective than those made by a team from sales, service, and manufacturing.

Selling *skill* is often transferable from one product or service to another as long as you can acquire the needed *knowledge*.

These skills—language, science and mathematics, computer competency, and sales—are just four broad examples of easily demonstrated hard skills.

Soft Skills. Unfortunately the woods are full of people with hard skills who can't function in organizations. Some have no interpersonal skills, while others trip over politics, and others cannot adjust to change.

Soft skills are less easy to define and prescribe, but can be every bit as important to your personal enterprise.

Interpersonal Skills. This can mean everything from your ability to communicate to your competence as a supervisor. Negotiating, building relationships, resolving conflict, and establishing a positive work climate are all examples of skills involving your interaction with other people.

Leadership is the most powerful and most written-about interpersonal skill. Many feel that leadership, like creativity, is in part a trait. That means that some of the behaviors can be learned, but effectiveness isn't assured.

Don't spend too much time on that debate. Rather, invest in gaining interpersonal skills because achievement of the goals in your plan for self-reliance will depend in great measure on your skills in dealing with others. Being self-reliant doesn't mean being a loner. Strategic alliances, support groups, partnerships, and even employment relationships may all be part of your strategy of self-reliance.

Team Skills. Whether you are a team member or leader, these skills are becoming increasingly valuable as more and more companies adopt this form of organization. Understanding group behavior, exerting influence in a group, and being able to adapt your goals to those of the group are typical team skills.

Because these teams can be self-managing, many of the self-reliant skills you develop as an individual will be needed by the team as a unit.

Revenue and Cost Focus. This isn't a new idea or skill, but it has now become identified as a separate and important one. Broadly defined, it means:

- Having the skill to see how your actions, no matter in what capacity, can increase revenue or lower costs
- Seeing the business from the eyes of the customer and applying creativity to satisfying customer needs
- Getting the most out of the resources you manage

To increase revenue and lower costs you need to understand how your company makes money. You need to know its objectives and strategies. To be most effective, your skills in this area will include a good understanding of what others do and how to work with them to achieve this focus.

Timely Decision Skills. These are essential to turn your revenue/cost focus into action. You need the skills to make correct decisions, normally a combination of gathering knowledge and applying analysis, and you need the skills to make decisions quickly. Organizational speed is now recognized as a strategic strength. Competitive battles are being won or lost on how quickly a product or service can be brought to market. Huge cost savings can come from shortening development time or reducing the time that money is owed. If you can contribute to that strength, you have additional in-demand skills.

Information Gathering. This is absolutely essential to decision making. While it is a soft skill, finding, retaining, and interpreting information takes hard work and a kind of resourcefulness that typifies the idea of self-reliance. The two variables to employing this skill are: (1) knowing what information to gather and (2) where to get it.

There is a trick to knowing what information to gather. The first step is not to ask what information is needed. Most people either won't know or will ask for far more information than they need. Tons of green-and-white-striped computer printouts languish around offices as proof. The trick is to determine what decisions you or others need to make, and work on getting the information required to make those decisions.

Where to get information depends on what it is and how important it is. Commissioning a major consulting study, visiting a competitor, doing a library literature search, or making a phone call to someone who has an answer to a question could all be appropriate at one time or another. The second trick to gathering information, then, is to cultivate as deep a file of resources as you can. If you've done a good job of identifying what information you need, building a resource file will be easier.

Political Skills. These have always been valuable, but with the advent of flatter, less formal hierarchies of decision making and power, your personal enterprise must be politically skilled. Political skills relate to your ability to understand and function in the culture and informal power structure of an organization. It's knowing which behaviors are and are not valued, what the standards are for appearance and work habits, and what the actual flow of information is and who influences that flow. The ultimate results of political activity are making and implementing decisions.

Observe and analyze decisions and how they were made. When a decision seems to be illogical, you may be missing the politics of it. Seek to understand who had what influence on the outcome and why.

Advice on this soft but often brutal skill has been written about in everything from Nicolo Machiavelli's *The Prince* to Susan Haden Elgin's *The Gentle Art of Verbal Self-Defense.*

Versatility. This is a skill requiring two components: broad competence and adaptability. If you make the investments to add a good mix of hard and soft skills, and to balance expertise with flexibility, you will add this valuable skill to your personal enterprise.

Other Soft Skills. You might want to develop competency in the realms of *quality* and *international business.* The focus on these two areas indicates they are trends, not fads.

ACTION STEP 44 *Develop a Plan to Acquire the Knowledge and Skills You Want*

Once you have chosen a strategy for investing in yourself and have decided what investments to make, it's time to decide how you will make those investments. You have a rich array of resources available to you. Some (like universities) are costly, while others (like libraries) are virtually free.

ACTION STEP 45 *Pursue Skills Acquisition through Institutions*

You can use a variety of institutions to help you acquire the skills you want.

High schools, colleges and universities offer full- and part-time programs, day and evening courses, credit and noncredit courses, and often offer special programs to meet specific needs of their market. Some institutions may specialize in your field.

A few learning institutions advertise and all have some form of catalog. Increasingly, they use direct mail to solicit enrollments, and you should get on the mailing lists of schools offering programs in your desired skills.

Private institutions such as computer centers or real estate schools offer specialized training, while some—like The Learning Annex or The California Institute of Integral Studies—offer courses in everything from filmmaking to flirting, all at very reasonable prices.

Look for private institutions in the Yellow Pages and get on their mailing lists.

The armed services have always offered training and a way to afford it. The period of service required of you need not be full-time or active duty. The armed services now offer programs which will build a fund for your tuition once you complete your service. The services do, of course, have an openly discriminatory, though completely understandable, hiring policy regarding age and physical fitness.

Government training programs are offered by cities, states, and the federal government. The U.S. Government Manual mentioned in Part 2 is a guide to federal programs. Federal training programs are the responsibility of the Department of Labor. Listed here are some specific programs, and the phone numbers to find more information about them:

Office of Trade Adjustment Assistance. This office oversees programs providing reemployment services such as training, job search and relocation allowances, and weekly cash payments to people who have lost their jobs because of foreign imports. (202) 523-0555.

Bureau of Apprenticeship and Training. This office oversees and promotes apprenticeship programs. (202) 535-0540.

Office of Job Training Programs. This office is responsible for administering the Job Training Partnership Act of 1982. The goal of the act is to train (or retrain) and place eligible individuals in permanent, unsubsidized employment, preferably in the private sector. (202) 535-0236.

Veterans' Employment and Training Service. The service directs programs through a nationwide network of field offices an in cooperation with the states. (202) 532-9116.

State and local programs can be found by contacting the appropriate employment office or an office of human resources development.

ACTION STEP 46   *Take Advantage of Work-related Training*

In addition to institutions, you have a rich source of training at your place of work, even if your company doesn't offer formal training programs. Don't wait for someone to offer training to you—take the initiative to find out what's available. If your company doesn't offer some training which you think it should, take the added initiative to propose a program as a suggestion.

Formal training is offered by many companies. Now that you know what knowledge and experience you want, you can take the initiative and seek out the programs that fit your plan. Don't overlook conferences and other similar events that you might be able to attend.

On-the-job training is a valuable and often overlooked way to get the experience you are after. You can ask to have responsibilities added to your job. Volunteer for special assignments, project teams, and task forces. One good way to do that is to identify a problem or opportunity which needs multiple skills to solve and, at the same time, identify the people (including yourself) who will be needed to do the job.

Create a rationale for cross-training with other people. Companies are (or should be) looking for ways to increase flexibility and keep head count low. Having people cross-trained in many skills and tasks is a good way to do it.

Seek out people in your company who might help you learn. Show your appreciation with lunch or a small gift. Spend your own unpaid time, if you must, to observe, ask questions, and learn. These are investments in your personal enterprise and will add to your self-reliance.

Apprenticeships offered by companies and unions are tried-and-true ways to invest in yourself. If you made the investments in basic skills, such as language and math, you should be able to compete well for entry into these programs.

ACTION STEP 47 *Apprentice Yourself to an Expert, Formally or Informally*

Finding mentors, people who are willing to invest time and effort in your development, requires that you find people whose own objectives complement yours. Finding people who would spend the time simply because they are altruistic would be serendipitous. More likely, you will find people who like you and who see in your potential the means to achieve their own or the company's goals.

The real challenge is not so much for you to find a mentor, but for a mentor to find you. Some techniques to help that happen are covered in Chapter 7, but the single best thing you can do is superlative work.

ACTION STEP 48 *Gain Knowledge and Skill on Your Own*

If you haven't spent much time learning on your own, you are in for a surprise. The marketplace for training, development, and self-improvement is huge. Seminars, tapes, books, products, courses, counseling, workshops, and retreats ranging from mountain climbing (to build your confidence) to isolation (to find your "center") are offered by companies and individuals.

You can find information about these offerings in advertisements in magazines and newspapers, and some will arrive via direct-mail campaigns. You can also contact the American Society for Training and Development* or the Human Resources Information Network,† which provide substantial databases of available programs.

Richard Bolles has assembled an extensive list of counseling resources at the back of his *What Color Is Your Parachute?*‡

Regulation in this marketplace, particularly in the self-help arena, is spotty, so shop very carefully. The promotional material is aimed at peoples' deepest needs for security and self-actualization, and some claims for success are wonderfully appealing. As usual, if something sounds too good to be true, it probably is.

Libraries deserve special mention. They, and to a lesser extent bookstores, are gold mines for people with the initiative to explore and exploit them. At little or no cost, you can have access to many of the same ideas, products, and services offered for sale in the market. More importantly, libraries organize information for you in exactly the way you are looking for it—by subject.

Libraries deserve special mention because of the developments in library technology in just the last few years. Most public and university libraries are now on computer systems, which give them—and you—access to materials in dozens of other libraries. Libraries are increasingly becoming subscribers to computerized on-line and CD ROM databases. This means you have access to millions of up-to-date facts on your subjects of interest.

And libraries are becoming increasingly active in career issues by taking initiatives to assemble resource lists, offering special speakers' programs, and becoming network centers.

Other learning on your own can include your reading program. To stay alert to your world, you need to read the right newspapers, books, and magazines. Taking an active part in your trade or professional association can help. By following the previous steps in developing your program for self-reliance, you now have a clear set of investment objectives, and this will help you focus your efforts.

* ASTD
1630 Duke Street
Alexandria, VA 22313

† Human Resources Information Network
9585 Valpariso Court
Indianapolis, IN 46268

‡ *What Color Is Your Parachute?*, Ten Speed Press, Berkeley, Calif.

ACTION STEP 49   *Get Help with Your Development Plan*

Expect to be pleasantly surprised when you seek help in preparing your development plan. Your boss and your company's human resources department are easy places to start. High schools and colleges have counseling help. Librarians can help. You can hire professionals from the list of resources mentioned elsewhere in this chapter. You might simply team up with others in your situation and be resources to each other in preparing your personal development plans.

The American characteristic of helping and even cheering those who are working to get ahead is still alive and well, as you will discover.

ACTION STEP 50   *Recognize That It's All up to You*

All the help and resources in the world, by themselves, can't make you more knowledgeable or more skilled, or make you more in demand. To be sure, serendipity and luck will play a part in your development, but luck only benefits the well-prepared.

Knowledge and skill cannot be built using excuses. If you can find the time to watch TV, you can find the time to take a course. If you don't have a lot of money, use the library and on-the-job training.

The Ultimate Value.   These investments may be hard to make. They may call for sacrifices in time, money, and effort. But they are investments in your own personal enterprise, investments in your skills and knowledge, that will provide you with something no one can take away from you—your self-reliance.

PART 4

The Subtle (and Not-So-Subtle) Art of Self-Promotion

. . . though the wide universe is full of good, no kernel of nourishing corn can come to him but through his toil . . .

RALPH WALDO EMERSON
essay on "Self-Reliance"

From the first page of this book you have been told that in-demand skills are necessary for your personal enterprise to succeed. Good work habits and job performance have also been mentioned as necessary elements for success. They are *necessary*, but they are not *sufficient* to guarantee your self-reliance.

To repeat the entire earlier phrase:

The best economic insurance you can obtain is having skills that are in demand *and having lots of employers, headhunters, and other influential people know* who you are, where you are, and how good you are.

What you *don't* want is to be out of a job and in the pack with others as they mass-mail résumés, chase the want ads, and network frantically. You need to insure against that risk by actively generating a steady flow of interest in your personal enterprise.

7

Get Sharp!
Get Recognized!
. . . and Make Job
Offers Come to You

Before we cover the many ways you can generate a flow of interest in your personal enterprise, you do need to understand the conventional ways to find a job.

ACTION STEP 51   *Learn the Basic Techniques of Job Search*

For years people in recruiting and outplacement have advocated four well-established methods of job search:

1. Responding to advertisements

2. Contacting executive recruiters

3. Contacting companies directly

4. Networking

Today we still use them, but with different emphasis and some new variations.

The current recession has dried up the normal formation and flow of job opportunities into the employment market. An obvious consequence is that *responding to ads* is less productive when there are fewer ads—and more applicants. *Recruiters* are a less fertile source for the same reason: their inventory of jobs is low. A less obvious factor impacting these two traditional methods is cost. Newspaper ads and recruiters are expensive, and many companies have a data bank of people on file and don't need help finding candidates.

Directly contacting companies and *networking* also suffer from the oversupply of applicants and scarcity of openings.

Substep 51.1   *Establish Objectives*

The first step in this process is to decide on an appropriate career direction. Earlier chapters have helped you sort through what is needed to set your direction. Once you decide on a career direction, you establish transition objectives—targets for the industries, positions, geographic areas, companies, and people you want to contact. Your job campaign strategy flows from these objectives.

The next step is to select your campaign method. Experts strongly advocate a balanced approach using all four campaign methods.

Substep 51.2   *Respond to Advertisements*

Competition when responding to ads makes it tough just to get attention, much less get a job. To get attention, you must be different. The best way to be different is to be interesting, and that means focusing on the issues of interest to the company or recruiting firm that placed the ad.

Carefully craft and tailor all ad responses to the specific ad. That means that you customize both your cover letter *and résumé* to match each ad.

Substep 51.3   *Convert Actions to Accomplishments and Experience to Results*

If the ad talks about "being a team player," you should find a way to talk not only about your experience being a team player but the results, too. The same goes for "cost-conscious," and the ubiquitous "results-oriented." Describe your actions, but highlight your accomplishments. If specific experience, skills, or education are mentioned, try to address them directly and positively. Customizing may require some homework. The more you know about the company and what it needs, the stronger your ad response can be.

To increase exposure, scan as many newspapers as possible, including several weeks of their back issues, to find additional appropriate ads.

Substep 51.4   *Contact Recruiters*

First, focus on recruiters who specialize in your industry or functional area. Use your networking to gain personal introductions to other recruiters. Today, you must be able to cultivate a personal relationship with recruiters, and that requires a focused program, not mass broadcast mailings. Plan to use periodic phone contact. Send clippings of your accomplishments, publications, and so on. Find ways you can be helpful to the recruiter, such as helping him or her get a search assignment.

Recruiters *do* need attractive candidates, but candidates must create the opportunity to meet with them. The competition is stiff to be on a recruiter's list.

Substep 51.5   *Contact Companies Directly*

You can bypass the crush of ad responders and the gauntlet of recruiters by contacting companies directly. This used to involve the drudgery of digging through directories by hand, copying names and addresses, and typing individual letters. Now you can use computerized databases of companies or other data sources to give you access to a broad universe. Here's what to do:

1. The first step is to target firms matching your established career options.

2. Next, learn all you can about the firm. Get an annual report if it's a public company. Read articles in newspapers and magazines to learn about issues. Search out financial results and the names of key people. The research may require the use of public or college libraries and may involve digging for information by phone.

3. Target specific people and, where possible, key in on real company issues as a way to stand out in today's crowded and competitive market.

Substep 51.6   *Network—But with Care*

Networking, the personal, direct marketing technique, is accepted as the most effective of the four job search methods. Today, though, even this channel is crowded with job seekers and others who are seeking opportunities.

Experts advocate targeting to focus on the best probable sources of job leads, and no longer recommend the cold call "information" contact to strangers unless the candidate has a special story to tell the person. People in hiring roles complain today about the number of phone calls they get from people who "just want to learn about your company."

Many people learned the old rules of networking:

1. Always view everybody as a potential network member.
2. Always be ready to network instantly.
3. Keep records on everyone you meet.
4. Put a tickler on your records and stay in touch with everyone.

Today, people recognize that the old rules lead to shallow and overloaded networks that do little to help you stay in demand. Most networks end up as little more than piles of business cards with notes scribbled on the back.

Networks now need to be managed by new rules:

1. View your network as a long-term commitment.
2. Carefully pick network members who can help you and whom you can help.
3. Build quality relationships, not quantity contacts.
4. Produce results for your network members and let them know how to produce results for you.

Start your network through friends, family, and others who know you and who will actively help. The surprise is how long and productive that list can be. (See pp. 104–107.)

The first objective is to learn about job opportunities from these people. The second objective is to ask these people for help in getting to the targeted contacts you want to reach. By bridging from someone known to the desired contact, you avoid the cold call.

ACTION STEP 52   *Employ a New Strategy for Today's Market—The Targeted Résumé "Job Proposal"*

A powerful new strategy is based on the "job proposal." Pure and simple, you develop a *business proposal* aimed at convincing a hiring manager in a specific company to create a position for you. The proposal requires research and creativity to know what problems and opportunities your target company most likely faces. A literature search and talking with people who know the company or the industry are two ways to learn. In your proposal, spell out the kind of job you envision and what your duties would be. Focus on how you can solve specific problems and, by doing so, how you can *increase revenue* or *reduce costs.*

To be most effective, you should use your network to arrange a personal introduction or at least a sponsored delivery of the job proposal.

This innovative approach distinguishes you from the crowded and competitive field of job seekers and makes you a potential problem solver. If the job proposal doesn't yield a permanent job, it may at least lead to project or consulting assignments which may be attractive.

Your search for a job requires extensive work to plan, implement, and control an effective campaign.*

ACTION STEP 53   *Don't Stop When You Find a Job*

Sad as it may seem, your new job may end up like your old one—cut back, out-sourced, or downsized. Keep your contacts alive. Update

---

* For more on job searching, visit your library or any major bookstore.

your résumé at once. By all means, treat your new job as though you will be there forever, but treat yourself as though it could be gone tomorrow.

ACTION STEP 54 *Learn to Promote Your Personal Enterprise*

If you are choosing the option of business ownership, much of what follows will still be of use to you, especially if your business is a consulting practice.

Promotion in this book has three components: *what* you are promoting, *to whom* you are promoting, and *how* you promote.

What You Are Promoting. What you are promoting is simply you—your personal enterprise, its accomplishments, its features, and its other interesting and unique facets. Most of all, you are promoting the ways that your personal enterprise can be of benefit to others. Most often, as I've said, the market value of your enterprise rests on your ability to increase revenue or reduce costs, but Figure 7-1 (repeated from Chapter 2) is a more expansive list of the benefits someone else might seek from you. The list is stated in terms of *needs*.

What you are promoting are your abilities to satisfy those needs.

To Whom Are You Promoting? Under some extraordinary conditions, everybody could be the target of your promotion, but that's unlikely. Some will be too indirectly connected to your objective and others may simply not be relevant. *The mistake most people make, however, is to consider too few people as promotional targets.*

Clearly Understand the Potentially Huge Size of Your Audience. Think for a moment how each of the following people just might help you stay in demand.

Your boss influences your job, your performance appraisal, your pay, your promotions, and your image. He or she will probably be a reference others inside and outside your company will want.

Other bosses may control the job you want. They may also have credibility as boosters or detractors of your image.

To increase sales
To save money
To save time
To save effort
To feel good
To be popular
To win praise
To gain recognition
To conserve possessions
To increase well-being
To be in style
To copy others
To protect a reputation
To avoid criticism
To avoid trouble
To profit from opportunities
To gain control over his or her life
To solve a problem
To be safe and secure
To please someone important
To end confrontation or sales pressure
To be different
To obey the law

Figure 7-1. Needs.

Co-workers (past and present), by virtue of their numbers, represent a large network of people who are in positions every day to see job openings, opportunities, and threats to your personal enterprise.

Recruiters are obvious targets for your promotional efforts. Most recruiters keep files on people they consider would make top candidates for assignments. Recruiters often specialize and take pride in knowing who are the top people in their field of specialization.

Employers in your industry may be the most important targets for you because your skills and knowledge should be worth more to them. However, they can't know who you are, where you are, and how good you are if someone doesn't tell them. Don't risk your personal enterprise on a hope that these important people will know about you.

Faculty members come into contact with lots of people and are credible references.

Employers in your area are vital to your personal enterprise if you need or want to stay in your area. The more limited the employer base, the more important your need to be known by them.

Public accountants and auditors deal with companies every day. They know which firms have problems and which have opportunities. Their recommendation carries a lot of weight with their clients.

Consultants are in much the same situation as public accountants; they spend their time with company managements who have confidence in them.

Bankers see many businesses and, like public accountants, know of opportunities and problems. Bankers, on occasion, know more and know sooner about *planned* activities, both good and bad. A banker's recommendation is a strong asset for your personal enterprise.

People in your industry who may not be actual employers, such as analysts, commentators, and regulators may still have valuable knowledge and powerful influence. Sometimes endorsement by one of these people can be compared to knighthood.

Professional associates know better than most anyone what you can do and what an appropriate opportunity would look like. These people do have to know what you want from them.

Civic club members are usually community activists who have diverse affiliations and broad spheres of influence. These are the people who could remark about you, "Oh, yes, I know that person from Rotary," or whatever the club.

Charitable organizations give you an opportunity to "do well by doing good." Your involvement will most certainly be welcome and your leadership and contribution will almost always give you positive visibility. Charity work attracts a circle of influential people.

Alumni, whether known to you or not, may have a loyalty to your school. That can be an opportunity for you if their loyalty is coupled with needs which match your career objectives.

Friends are an overlooked resource. You might assume your friends know exactly what your career plan is and that they would always be alert for opportunities on your behalf. Don't risk that assumption. People sometimes don't want to burden friends. That's another assumption you should test.

Neighbors, like friends, are often overlooked because people fail to see them in any other context.

Classmates are recognized as a resource, but all too often the only time classmates hear from one of their own is when the person is out of work and wants help. If you practice the art of self-promotion well, your classmates will see any call for help on your part as justified. If your self-promotion is successful, they will already be helping you.

Media people can be the hardest to reach but the easiest to leverage. One mention in *Business Week, The Wall Street Journal,* or even your local paper can mean instant visibility, and possibly celebrity.

Customers can tell you what's going on in the marketplace. With little effort, they can make you known to others in your trade. Customers are your link to other parts of your industry.

Suppliers are another link to other parts of your industry and another resource who can easily refer you to key people.

Dentists and doctors should be seen as the helping professionals they are. As such, they are almost always well disposed to help you in other parts of your life.

Clergy have a broader role as helping professionals and have emerged as leaders in helping people with career support. In parts of the country, the clergy actively manage career networks and transition centers.

Fellow commuters are natural targets for your self-promotion. Common experience, along with diversified contacts, can mean strong mutual benefits among commuters.

Competitors should see the most value in who you are, but sometimes they and you are prohibited, ethically or legally, from being in contact.

People who promote to you are in the same marketplace in at least one way. They can be good network contacts.

Make up your personal list adding others and giving at least some general priority to them to your targets.

How to Promote Yourself.   Working in or observing public relations and advertising are as close as most people get to seeing the techniques of promotion. Even then, the parallels with personal promotion aren't apparent because PR and advertising typically promote a product or service.

Major political elections give you some insight into a narrow, media-focused type of publicity being used as part of a full personal promotional campaign.

You have many more ways to promote your personal enterprise. Your challenge is to construct your program of self-promotion so that it does what you want it to do. That means setting some objectives.

Objectives for your self-promotion could include any of the following:

- getting in print
- getting considered for future jobs
- creating favorable awareness
- overcoming a bad image or event
- doing a favor/creating an obligation or appreciation
- getting an introduction to someone
- getting recommended
- establishing yourself as an expert
- showing appreciation
- getting money
- gaining professional status
- getting a promotion or raise
- creating a "fan club"
- gaining visibility
- attracting a mentor
- getting elected or chosen

With your targets in sight and your objectives set, you are ready to build your plan for self-promotion using the techniques best suited to your needs.

Techniques.   Tips 55 through 78 offer a "menu" of 25 techniques which successful self promoters recommend to help you stay in demand.* You may not be able (or willing) to use all of them, but the mistake most people make is not using enough of them. *Many peo-*

---

*For an in-depth look at media self-promotion see *The Unabashed Self-Promoter's Guide* by Dr. Jeffrey Lant, Jeffrey Lant Associates, Cambridge, Mass.

ple do absolutely no self-promotion of their personal enterprise. Imagine what that would do to a conventional business. Imagine, too, what advantages your competitors have if they are promoting.

ACTION STEP 55   *Prepare to Promote*

You will need to prepare for your promotional activities. If you don't have business cards or if you want cards that don't present your employer's name, get your own. They can be very plain with just your name, address, and phone number, but get high-quality cards. Apply the same standards to your personal stationery.

Determine how you will handle secretarial functions. If you can't handle them on your own, you can hire secretarial services, or perhaps pay a friend. If the load is going to be heavy or of critical importance to your personal enterprise, you may want to invest in acquiring your own capabilities. Consider whether you will need an answering machine.

Make your introductions memorable. (See the two-minute drill on p. 122.)

ACTION STEP 56   *Initiate Your Own Performance Review*

Waiting for an annual review of your performance or some random feedback on what the boss thinks of you is a passive and risky use of your career time. One or a series of *self-initiated performance reviews* (SIPR) can help you stay in control of this critical relationship.

As the name implies, these sessions will have you proposing, asking, or confirming what's expected from you and seeking your boss's agreement.

The first step toward a self-initiated performance review is to gain the boss's agreement to the idea. It's hard to imagine a boss who would not respond positively to your suggestion of something that will help performance.

You have two objectives for your SIPR: receiving information and gaining positive visibility.

Your declared intent for the meeting is to review your job performance. If you have an agreed-upon set of objectives with your boss, present the progress you have made toward those goals. If you don't have stated mutual objectives, offer the objectives you have set for yourself and present your progress toward them. Try to quantify your results in terms of higher revenue or lower cost. "Conducted xyz survey" may be what you did, but "Conducted xyz survey which led to a four-day reduction in accounts receivable" is what you want to convey to show the value of your personal enterprise.

ACTION STEP 57   *Understand What Others Want and Expect*

Use the SIPR to learn what your company and your boss believe is important to them. Understand their objectives, problems, and opportunities. Ask about specific ways they are trying to increase revenue or reduce costs, and listen for opportunities for your personal enterprise to take on those tasks.

Then ask (and suggest) how you can best contribute to those tasks. Put your formal job description aside. Ask to take on the task that will contribute most to your boss's and the company's objectives. These are your personal enterprise's most important clients.

This is also the time to ask for assignments which will broaden your knowledge and contribute to your development.

ACTION STEP 58   *Milk Meetings for All They're Worth*

For some nose-to-the-grindstone employees, attending meetings, conventions, and shows is a distracting waste of time. For people promoting their personal enterprise, these activities can be gold mines of opportunity to learn, to grow, and to meet people.

The actual content of these events may or may not be of particular value to your personal enterprise, but events around them are often useful. Social activities and seminar sessions will bring you into contact with people in your field—people who should know who you are, where you are, and how good you are. Even the attendance list can contain a wealth of contact names for you.

No judgment is made here on the subject of mutual loyalty between companies and employees. Let duty, ethics, and just plain fairness keep you from taking advantage of your employer.

ACTION STEP 59 *Make Organizational Membership a Platform for Getting Known*

The two considerations for effective organization membership are to choose organizations which can truly benefit you and to work hard for the organizations you join.

Choose organizations which have objectives connected to yours, which have members with whom you wish to associate, and which can provide you with opportunities for visibility.

Contribute to your organization. Hard work and worthwhile results are the underpinnings for effective promotion, just as they are for any undertaking.

ACTION STEP 60 *Assume Leadership in Organizations*

One high-visibility job in organizations, committees, and task forces is to be the secretary. The secretary can influence the agenda, has access to membership rolls, and gains notice as the signatory to meeting notices and minutes. In his or her role as the group's communicator, the secretary is often afforded direct contact with members.

ACTION STEP 61 *Work at Everyday Communications and Social Activity*

It may seem calculating to keep and refer to lists of people's birthdays or their children's names. You may find it hard to put people on a "contact schedule" to ensure that they remember you. Using social activity to further your personal enterprise may make you feel like a user.

As long as you have no intention of taking advantage of people and are perfectly willing to reciprocate, you might view these actions at better, more purposeful communications as simply another skill which you need to develop and use.

Insincere, programmed, and inappropriate communications will be recognized by people for the pro forma activity it is. Your good judgment will announce to you when your self-promotion activities need to be overt or subtle, and when they need to be put aside altogether.

ACTION STEP 62   *Cultivate a Genuine Interest in Others*

Your communications, networking, and other self-promotion activities will make you feel less selfish if you can cultivate real interest in others. No one can make you feel interest, but you can develop the skills to learn about people, to understand them, to appreciate their differences, to find out about their goals, fears, problems, opportunities, and even their dreams. People are interesting. If you open yourself up to this kind of exploration and make the learning investment, you stand a good chance of developing interest in others.

ACTION STEP 63   *Get Involved in Political Activity*

Holding office or serving on boards will bring you a very high level of recognition, but there are other kinds of political involvement. You can be active in party activities such as fund-raising, hosting events, or serving on committees.

A bonus of your involvement in political activity is that politics is a popular subject for press coverage and a natural arena for networking.

ACTION STEP 64   *Take Part in Charity and Other Volunteer Work*

A person can "do well by doing good," so it is said. Choose the organizations you want to work with on the basis of mutual benefit. You must be willing to contribute the time, effort, and other resources the organization needs for you to expect to receive the benefit you want.

You will gain the most visibility if you serve in leadership roles. For example, being responsible for the group's publicity will put you in contact with members of the media.

This method of gaining recognition has one big advantage, because these organizations will gladly accept your active involvement. If your involvement gets visibility for you, it gets visibility for the organization, too.

ACTION STEP 65   *Get Quoted*

If you've ever wondered how some people seem to get calls constantly from publications and end up being quoted, wonder no more. They don't get calls out of the blue, they work at it very purposefully.

No matter what your field, there are journals, magazines, house organs, or newsletters which act as forums for ideas and commentary. If your field is broad, national publications like *Business Week* and *The Wall Street Journal* might be relevant.

Getting quoted requires three things:

1. Having something worth quoting
2. Finding out who might quote you
3. Making sure those who might quote you know about you

Substep 65.1   *Have Something Worth Quoting*

It's been suggested that you develop some special expertise. If you did, you have built an inventory of facts, experiences, opinions, and ideas in your expert domain. Here's a golden chance to use them to gain recognition and credibility.

Start by analyzing what topics in your field are hot topics of discussion. Maybe it's a new technological breakthrough, a piece of pending legislation, a need to reduce costs, a new competitive pressure, or even some issue of style, trend, or taste. Pore over your relevant publications and, if it's appropriate, the radio and television shows that cover your field, and find something in your expert domain that's getting heavy coverage.

The next step is to develop something quotable. For a quote to be interesting, it should not only add to the body of knowledge, it should offer something fresh, and have an unusual insight or slant. It might point out something that was missed in previous coverage of the subject.

If you think you have a problem writing or clearly expressing your quotable thoughts, get some help. Read a book. Take a course—you need writing skills to ensure you can exploit your full employment value. If all else fails, hire a writer.

Substep 65.2 *Find Out Who Might Quote You*

Finding out who might quote you is really straightforward detective work. When you read articles that have a writer's byline, put the writer's name in your database. If there is no byline, call or write the publication and find out who wrote the piece.

In the case of trade publications where the whole magazine or newsletter is on your topic, get the names of the editorial staff, starting with the editor. For radio and television, you need the name of the show's producer.

You may have opportunities to be quoted in your local press, which would have an interest in you as a local expert on almost any subject. Find out who on the local paper covers your subject or your area.

You can get ideas and help from *Writer's Market,** which contains over 4000 listings of book, magazine, periodical, and trade journal editors, and from *Editor & Publisher Yearbook,*[†] which lists editors and publishers from nearly every newspaper in the world.

Substep 65.3 *Make Sure Those Who Might Quote You Know about You*

Nearly all working writers and editors keep a file of experts on whom they call to verify facts, get ideas, and generally deepen their understanding of a subject. You have to get your name into that file and keep it there. That means you have to let the appropriate person know who you are and what your expert domain is. Use the telephone, a letter, or some combination to make the first contact and offer a quotable observation on your subject. Describe your qualifications as an expert and your continuing pursuit of the subject. Offer to be of help any time the writer/editor is covering the subject.

---

* *Writer's Market* (annual), Writer's Digest Books, Cincinnati, Ohio, edited by Glenda Neff.

[†] *Editor & Publisher Yearbook* (annual), Editor & Publisher Co., New York.

Follow up this initial contact with a purposeful program of ongoing communications. Give the writer/editor feedback. They, like all of us, enjoy receiving compliments on their work. Drop notes and comments to the writer/editor about trends you see, experiences and events, and other observations which you think would be of interest.

Repeat this process with others: other writers, others who speak on your topic, association executives, academics, researchers, and anyone else who might just pick up the phone and ask you for your (quotable) thoughts.

If this seems like a lot of effort, remember this: once you're quoted, the more likely you are to be quoted again. When you're quoted several times, you become an expert. Your name, when quoted as an expert, is what others clip and file and use as a source when they want an expert. In a relatively short time, this one self-promotion technique can catapult you into stardom and really put you in demand.

ACTION STEP 66 *Write Articles (or Even Letters) That Get Noticed*

As an expert, you can do more than get quoted, you can get published. Select your target publications and your topic using the same techniques mentioned in "Get Quoted" (Action Step 65).

Do some research on the publications you have targeted. Learn their style and format. Uncover the names of the editors and their area of responsibility. *Writer's Market* and *Editor & Publisher* can be very helpful. Above all, *get to understand their readers* and what the readers want. Editors view everything that comes across their desks with an eye to their readers. If you appear to not understand the readers, you run a near-certain risk of having your submission rejected.

The accepted procedure to get published in a periodical starts with a query letter* sent to the editor responsible for your subject area. In the query letter you will outline your idea for a proposed article and state your qualifications to write it. Explain briefly how

* *Writer's Market* and back issues of *Writer's Digest* magazine contain sample query letters.

you will approach your subject and, most important, why it should appeal to the readers. Double-space any sample material you submit. If you have been published previously, say so.

Some busy editors receive an avalanche of mail, so make things easy for them by enclosing a self-addressed stamped envelope.

If you receive the assignment, get clear guidance on the length desired and the due date. Have the editor describe what he or she wants the article to do, or what special focus is wanted. If you have concerns about your writing style, ask about ways the editor might help you.

If the publication pays for submissions like yours, consider it a bonus.

ACTION STEP 67 *Provide High-Visibility Pro Bono Consulting*

This is another way to do well by doing good. Churches, schools, hospitals, and other community service organizations need advice and help to solve problems and operate more effectively. Your personal enterprise has skills and knowledge that can be useful to them.

Apply the criteria of mutual benefit mentioned previously to choose the institutions. Research them to uncover the kinds of opportunities and problems they face. Determine how your expertise can be applied to them. Use the best combination of direct contact and networking to approach them and offer a proposal of help. Don't be overly specific; you need to hear from them what they see as their key needs.

Your work will provide benefit to the organizations, so be sure about how you will get from the opportunity the visibility you want.

ACTION STEP 68 *Become a Lecturer*

Public speaking isn't for everybody but, with some training, most people can learn to address an audience. Many of the institutions mentioned in Chapter 6 offer public-speaking courses. The potential to gain recognition for your personal enterprise by lecturing is not limited to your business or professional expertise. Your travels, hobbies, collections, and personal experiences may be of real interest to many groups.

Once again, you will do research and planning to secure lecture assignments. Decide on which groups you want to reach. Find out if they use (or would use) guest lecturers, and develop a list of lecture topics you could deliver to them. Lecturing to a group which can't help you is a waste of your time, and lecturing on a topic of no interest to a group is a waste of its time.

Use direct contact and networking to reach the groups you have chosen. If the group has other chapters or units, it may be an easy matter to arrange for more than one lecture engagement.

Professional lecturers advise an excellent way to gain more assignments. They urge you to conclude each talk with a statement to the audience that you are excited about your topic and that you would be pleased to present it to other interested groups.

You may want to consider giving public lectures if your subject has broad enough interest and your skills are well enough refined. You can use the aforementioned techniques to gain media publicity, but you may need to advertise or use direct marketing to get attendees.

ACTION STEP 69 *Create or Participate in Seminars*

Developing your expertise continues to be a cornerstone in your plan for self-reliance and to stay in demand. Once developed, your expertise can qualify you to be a panelist in seminars. Because you can be one of several participants, this is an easy way to get your feet wet and to learn how to be in front of an audience.

Your industry, professional, or trade associations are good places to look for existing seminar opportunities. Start a file on all the seminars in your field and make note of the names of the organizers. Contact them and offer to be a panelist.

Of course, you can develop seminars to offer through your associations or to offer on your own. You may want to have other panelists join you. You may even wish to develop public seminars, much as you might develop public lectures previously mentioned.

ACTION STEP 70 *Develop and Teach Courses on Your Specialty*

Many of the institutions mentioned in Chapter 6, as well as your own company, may have a desire to offer courses in your area of expertise. Your programs can be from one day to a full semester in length. You may be able to gain some accreditation for your program to add to its value.

Take the same initiatives described earlier to approach the key decision makers with a proposal.

Teaching lends credibility to your personal enterprise and affords added ways to gain visibility, often supported by the institution offering your program.

ACTION STEP 71 *Create, Conduct, and Publicize Surveys*

Surveys are often *marketing* programs, not educational exercises. A customer satisfaction survey may show brand A to be the most preferred. An industry survey of problems shows a high incidence of a problem which product X solves. It's likely that brand A and product X sponsored or conducted those surveys as another way to promote their products.

Your surveys can be more subtle. Your objective is self-promotion, not the sale of a product, and recognition can be achieved simply by providing useful information to people. Begin by deciding what information your promotional targets want or need. If you don't know, ask them. Give them a list of topics in your area of expertise that you think might be of interest to them. Tell them that you plan a series of informational communications and want to know their interests. Ask them to rank the topics "much interest," "some interest," or "no interest." This will help you set priorities.

Next, structure questions to develop the data to answer those questions. You can conduct your survey by researching literature or by interrogating people by mail, by phone, or in person. You can survey individuals or groups. Your survey can be highly focused, somewhat structured, or totally open-ended, depending on the data you need. Finally, write up the results of your survey in a way that your targets will find useful and will enjoy.

If you've done the work suggested here to cultivate editors and publishers, you may be able to get your survey published. Your credibility is enhanced by authoring a survey, further increased by having it published, and bolstered over and over by the use of reprints.

ACTION STEP 72   *Give Gifts, Mementos, Books, etc.*

Buying recognition through the giving of gifts can be risky and costly, but it is something you can carefully control. With good manners and common sense, it can be very effective.

The keys to successful giving are appropriateness and timeliness. Appropriateness means that your gift is in good taste, is something that the other person will appreciate, and is relevant to your relationship. Good manners dictate that your gifts be neither so meager that they embarrass nor so lavish that they obligate.

Timeliness is important because it can influence the perception of your motivation for gift giving. Don't try to deceive people about your motivation—most will know you are trying to build goodwill with them, but don't make your motivation appear like bribery because of poor timing. Giving a gift just before an event where the recipient can do something to benefit you is shallow and ill-advised. Giving a gift after you have received help can be viewed simply as proper appreciation.

ACTION STEP 73   *Clip and Send Articles of Interest*

Clipping and sending articles from newspapers and periodicals is an easy and inexpensive way to gain and maintain visibility with others. It involves—and shows—personal effort on your part. To enhance the personal touch, handwrite a note to send along with the clipping.

Common sense is again your guide. Sending articles that your recipient has likely already seen should be done only if you are offering some comment or analysis along with it. Sending too many clippings makes your purpose look superficial. Send clippings that will be useful and interesting.

However, don't be overly shy in sending clippings about yourself. Reasonable pride in an accomplishment is acceptable to most people.

ACTION STEP 74 *Publicize! Promote Your Family, Pets, Home, Food, Hobbies, Clothes, Travels, and More!*

Dr. Jeffrey Lant, author of *The Unabashed Self-Promoter's Guide,* offers detailed advice for avid self-promoters to turn nearly every aspect of their lives into media events. In one example, he cites how you could author an article about your spouse's fabulous chocolate cookies and get it published in the food section of your newspaper. Here are some outcomes from that effort:

- promotion of the cookies
- increased standing for your spouse
- a nice plug for you and your company, product, or service.

His suggested use of other family members and lifestyle habits follows similar guidelines.

The promotion of your personal enterprise is essential to achieve self-reliance. Dr. Lant believes that you should leave no stone unturned.

As outrageous as this tip might sound, the nub of the idea is that opportunities to get publicity are everywhere. Dr. Lant refers to himself and others who follow his ideas as "shameless" self-promoters, but a greater shame might lie in failing to promote your personal enterprise.

ACTION STEP 75 *Use Targeted Audience Networking*

You, like others, may feel that networking, expanding your circle of personal contacts by purposefully asking for introductions and leads, has been overdone. Strangers calling strangers asking for favors and advice *has* been overdone, and the abuses have generated resentment toward the whole idea of networking. In many cases, the whole exercise is wasted because the object of the contact isn't really able to be of any help anyway.

Networking, done properly, is still the most powerful technique to gain recognition. Networking can get you the contacts you need for other kinds of self-promotion in the media, the business community, and elsewhere.

Individual Networking.   Good networking takes good manners. More than mere politeness, good manners means that you have consideration for the people with whom you are dealing. Contact them at sensible times, always ask for their permission to continue the contact, have the courtesy to know something about them, make only appropriate inquiries, and, most of all, have some idea of how to reciprocate the help you are seeking. Reciprocation can range from helping your contacts get introductions they want to giving them business. I've heard of one appreciative networker who made a contribution to his contact's favorite charity.

Kate Wendleton, founder of the New York–based "Five O'Clock Club," a job search network, strongly advises networkers to avoid most of the kind of wholesale, shotgun networking aimed at one-time benefits. She recommends building *and then maintaining* genuine, longer-lasting networks based on mutual benefits.

It may seem to you that these approaches take too much time, but you can squander far more time flitting around dozens and dozens of hard-to-maintain, marginally helpful, possibly resentful contacts.

Group Networking—"Tips" Groups and "Leads" Groups. Some groups exist for the sole purpose of networking. These are not civic or professional groups, which are discussed subsequently, but, rather, groups whose primary goal is the promotion of members' wants and needs for contacts.

Transition support groups, many promoted by churches, exist to help people make job contacts. Long-term relationships among the group members are neither sought nor expected.

"Tips" groups or "leads" groups are relatively new kinds of networks designed to generate business leads for their members. Typically, 25 or so *noncompetitors* meet weekly to exchange very specific information about business activity and opportunities for the group's members. One member might ask another for an introduction to a desired potential customer. Members ask for help finding suppliers and employees. Continued membership in the group often requires a certain level of activity and contribution.

ACTION STEP 76   *Master Memorable Introductions—"The Two-Minute Drill"*

Skilled group networkers know they don't have much time to make a clear, memorable, and *useful,* impression on people. They have devised "the two-minute drill," which is a well-thought-out minipresentation of who they are, what they do, the kinds of help they are seeking, and the kinds of help they can provide. The drill may not always be two minutes. The presentation is tailored to each situation and person, but the networkers have the ideas and words well defined in their heads at all times.

One standard closing to these encounters has you exchanging business cards. Experienced networkers immediately—and in plain view—write on the back of the card to capture reminders of the conversation, the person, and any planned follow-up.

Another standard closing is "Do you know anyone who . . .", which is how networkers make new connections.

Whether you are networking formally or just meeting people, your skill at the two-minute drill can be a useful technique to promote your personal enterprise.

ACTION STEP 77   *Create Your Own Self-Promotion Network*

You can even start a network group. Think of three people who have similar, but not conflicting, objectives to promote their own personal enterprises. Meet with them and explore the idea of associating for the purpose of supporting and helping each other.

If practical, each of you could invite two or three others, until you have the size group you think will be most effective.

Help in the beginning might include giving each other ideas and developing self-promotion programs. More specific cooperation could take the form of help with introductions, support for club membership or public office, and direct assistance in calling each other to the attention of the public or the specific target of your self-promotion. Throwing a party in your own honor is easier if someone else makes all the arrangements.

An added value of a personal self-promotion network is that individual members can better avoid the risk of appearing too pushy, crass, or ill-mannered by openly promoting themselves. As each others' "press agents," network members can make far more direct and favorable comments about each other than they could make about themselves.

Your self-promotion network can become the equivalent of a trade association for your personal enterprise.

ACTION STEP 78 *Integrate Your Self-Promotion Activities*

Your objectives, targets, and techniques for self-promotion will overlap. Minimize duplication, avoid omissions, and make your efforts most efficient by developing an integrated plan. One useful device for integrating multipart plans is the matrix. Construct a self-promotion matrix by listing your targets down the left side and your techniques across the top. If you list your most important targets and objectives first, the upper part of your matrix will give you a good focus on your priorities. In the boxes formed by the matrix, put the specific action you plan to take.

Remember to include your place of employment as a target. Try to ensure that the recognition you earn outside earns recognition for you inside your firm as well.

The matrix will reveal gaps, duplication, and excesses in your efforts. You should be able to see how one technique might be broadened to meet several objectives or to reach more than one target. Evaluate the costs and benefits of your activities and the matrix will show you whether you have placed your efforts on your priorities.

The matrix elements can be transferred into a calendarized plan to give you an event/work schedule.

Finally, the matrix will show you the effort—or lack of it—you are giving to promoting your personal enterprise and building your self-reliance.

PART 5

Creating Security for Your Personal Enterprise

So use all that is called Fortune. Most men gamble with her, and gain all and lose all, as the wheel rolls.

RALPH WALDO EMERSON
essay on "Self-Reliance"

By now, you realize that you no longer can expect to have continued, uninterrupted, corporate employment. Chances are you will, at some time, be unemployed or self-employed. That means you need to provide security for your personal enterprise.

ACTION STEP 79 *Prepare Yourself for the Possibility of Unemployment or Self-Employment*

You build a secure foundation for your personal enterprise by developing and implementing three strategies: legal strategies, financial strategies, and personal wellness strategies.

Self-reliance does not mean doing everything yourself, as I've said. These important strategies will be wrought from complex, technical issues which change with external events and with your own changing situation. Unless you are an expert in these disciplines, use the professional help available.

ACTION STEP 80 *Assemble a Team of Advisers*

At a minimum, your team will need a lawyer, an accountant, an insurance agent, and a physician. You may want to add a financial planner, a banker, a fitness adviser, and a member of the clergy.

Use two criteria to select your advisers: *competence* and *willingness*.

Competence. All professionals are not equally competent, and most specialize in some aspect of their profession. The lawyer who handled your real estate closing may not be experienced in estate planning, while the accountant who does your taxes may not be familiar with small business bookkeeping practices.

Your objective is to have the resources, the ability, and the flexibility to manage your personal enterprise as an employee, an independent contractor, or a business owner. You need to prepare for employment, self-employment, and even unemployment. Your advisers need the expertise relevant to your objective.

A simple way to evaluate the competence of prospective advisers is to describe your objective to them and ask about their experience in helping others with similar objectives. Ask if you can speak with some of their other clients.

Your friends, other professionals, and business owners in your area may know or recommend competent advisers.

Willingness. Not all professionals want to work in this arena. The problems are uncommon, the effort is significant, and the responsibility is profound. Be sure your advisers want to work with you.

Ask about how they do their jobs, their hours of availability, and their billing rates and practices.

Ideally, your advisers should lend enthusiasm and support while at the same time providing sound advice and protection.

Achieving your objectives may take the coordinated work of more than one adviser. Preparing an estate plan is a good example that may involve your accountant, your attorney, and your insurance agent working together. Get them to know each other so that they become a team for you.

Managing Your Advisers. After you have selected your advisers, record their names, addresses, and phone numbers (including home phone numbers) and keep them handy at all times. It's normal to need advice in a hurry.

Remember that these are your advisers and that they work for you. Many nonprofessionals *abdicate* rather than *delegate* to professionals. Self-reliance depends on using good advice, not on uncritical acceptance of any advice given by a professional.

One long-established technique in managing professionals is to never ask *if* something can be done, but instead to ask *how* something can be done. Another method of management is to ask for more than one alternative solution or proposal. Ask about the merits and the risks of each alternative.

Substep 80.1 *Don't Become a Hostage to Your Advisers' Expertise*

You need not become an attorney or an accountant but you should learn enough about law and finance to perceive risks and opportunities for your personal enterprise. For example, an elementary understanding of contracts and of financial terminology is essential to your self-reliance, as is an awareness of the purposes of basic types of insurance policies.

Read, and organize yourself and your records. Libraries, bookstores, and courses, as well as the many other information sources given in Chapter 6, can help you gain the knowledge you need to manage your advisers.

8

Develop Your Legal Strategy

Americans are more litigious than any other people, possibly because we have more attorneys than do any other people. You may have already had a minor disagreement escalate into a lawsuit, or may have found yourself forced to use the legal system as a result of a frivolous suit against you.

It comes as a surprise to people that others can launch legal attacks which must be defended regardless of the merit of the argument. It comes as a greater surprise that arguments of little or no apparent merit can be successful. "The uncertainties of litigation" is an oft-used phrase that describes well the sometimes capricious behavior of courts, judges, and juries. While there is no guaranteed way to avoid legal entanglement for your personal enterprise, there are precautions and initiatives you can take.

ACTION STEP 81   *Conduct a Review of Your Legal Situation*

You and your attorney, along with your insurance agent (where appropriate), can conduct a review of your legal situation to determine your exposures or opportunities. Begin with a review of all contracts to which you are a party. This includes your mortgage or rental agreement and your employment agreement—whether written or not. List all other agreements and obligations, including those for

129

which you are a cosignor or guarantor. Identify those which might subject you to liens.

Tell your advisers about any disputes in which you are or may become involved.

If you serve on the boards of corporations or serve as a trustee for nonprofit groups, review your responsibilities with your advisers. Don't overlook your service on local elected boards and commissions.

Review all the present and planned activities of your personal enterprise. Pay particular attention to any potential for conflict of interest with your present employer.

Conduct a full credit investigation to check on the accuracy of your records. If you are already incorporated, check those legal and credit records, too. Fully disclose the amount, terms, and status of your debts.

The purpose of examining each of these elements and others you may add is first to determine your legal and financial exposure. In some cases it may be more and in others less than you thought. The degree of your exposure and the existence of opportunities will suggest the action to be taken.

Figure 8-1 presents the most typical legal encounters you might anticipate.

ACTION STEP 82 *Construct the Elements of Your Legal Strategy*

The ultimate purpose of your legal review is to create an explicit legal strategy which supports whatever objectives you have for your personal enterprise while it keeps your risks and exposures at an acceptable level.

A good legal strategy, then, should *protect* and *enable*.

Protection in a legal strategy is provided by the specific actions chosen to address each area of exposure. You may choose to *eliminate* a risk by eliminating the exposure, say, by resigning from a high-risk board. You may choose to *reduce* a risk by, for example, renegotiating the terms of an agreement. Or you may chose to *insure* against a risk by buying a policy or a bond.

You may need to resolve some areas of exposure through litigation or other means. Others may be "sleeping dogs," best left to lie.

Liability: Actions revolving around the responsibility you and your family/employees have to conduct yourselves so as not to damage others. Your responsibility extends to the products and services you provide.

Indebtedness: Controversy over the collection or payment of money owed, including debt restructuring and bankruptcy.

Fiduciary: Controversy arising from any special obligations to guard the welfare of others, such as service on representative boards, work as treasurer, and acting as a trustee.

Regulation: Disputes about conformance with codes, licensing agencies' rules, and special practices and procedures.

Contract performance: Disagreements between the parties to an agreement.

Real estate: Disagreements over this special kind of agreement and the associated matters of title.

Personal matters: Issues arising from divorce, estates, and similar affairs, as well as small claims and traffic encounters.

Figure 8-1. Typical legal exposures of your personal enterprise.

Initiating a specific strategy puts you in control and gives your personal enterprise its best degree of protection.

Enabling you to pursue your objectives involves the selection of the legal form of your enterprise and the satisfaction of all legal and regulatory requirements.

ACTION STEP 83 *Choose a Legal Form for Your Personal Enterprise*

You can choose from five legal forms:

1. Independent contractor or sole proprietorship
2. General partnership

3. Limited partnership

4. Subchapter "S" corporation

5. "C"-type corporation

Table 8-1 compares these forms along several considerations.

Once you have chosen the form of your personal enterprise, all that remains is to be sure you satisfy such requirements as licensing, bonding, reporting, and any special fiduciary regulations. You can learn about these special requirements from your advisers and from others who are in the same field that you plan to enter.

Table 8-1. Legal Forms of Organization

Consideration	Sole proprietorship	Partnership		Corporation	
		General	Limited	C corporation	S corporation
Complexity of formation and operation	Simple	Relatively simple most of the time, written agreement preferable	More complex, requires written agreement and state filing of officers and directors, etc.	Most complex, requires state charter, election	Same as a C corporation in legal operation and formation
Limits on numbers of owners or shareholders	1	Unlimited	Unlimited	Unlimited	Limited to 35 shareholders
Owners' personal liability for business debts and claims of litigation	Unlimited personal liability	Unlimited personal liability	Unlimited personal liability for general partners; generally limited to amount of investment for limited partners	Generally not liable for corporate debts, with a potential exception for Federal withholding taxes	Same as a C corporation
Federal income taxation of business profits	Taxes paid by owner at individual rates	Taxes paid by partner at individual rates	Taxes paid by partner at individual rates	Taxes paid by corporation at corporation rates	Taxes paid by shareholders at at individual rates
Deduction of business losses by owners	Yes, provided active participation by owner	Yes, but limited to amounts personally at risk and passive loss rules	Yes, but limited to amounts personally at risk and passive loss rules	No	Yes, but limited to investment in stock and loans to the corporation; also subject to passive loss rules

Table 8-1. Legal Forms of Organization (Continued)

Consideration	Sole proprietorship	Partnership		Corporation	
		General	Limited	C corporation	S corporation
Taxation of dividends or other withdrawals of profits	No	No	No	Yes	No
Social security tax on owners' earnings	15.30% (12.40% OASDI + 2.90% hospital insurance) OASDT up to $55,500 of earnings hospital insurance up to $130,000	Same as sole proprietor	No	15.30% (12.40% OASDI + 2.90% hospital insurance) OASDT up to $55,500 of earnings hospital insurance up to $130,000	Same as C corporation
Unemployment taxes	No	No	No	Yes, both federal and state generally	Yes, both federal and state generally
Availability of deductible qualified deferred compensation plans for retirement	Yes, however borrowing prohibited by owner-employee	Yes, however borrowing prohibited by 10% partner	No	Yes, including the ability to borrow	Yes, however borrowing prohibited by 5% shareholder/employee
Medical, disability, and group term life insurance on owners	Generally not deductible; however, medical insurance is as medical expense in excess of 7.5% adjusted gross income	Same as sole proprietor	Same as sole proprietorship	Corporation deduction generally not taxable to employer under certain conditions	Generally not deductible if paid for a 2% or more shareholder—same as sole proprietorship

Available options of reporting year	Limited to calendar year	Must conform to year end of majority partners	Same as general partnership	Any 12-month period, except for personal service corporations	Must conform to year-end of majority shareholders (exception provided for natural business year)
Ability to allocate income among several owners	No	Yes	Yes	No	Yes
Automobile expenses	Deductible to the extent of 80% of ordinary and necessary expenses of carrying on a trade or business; maintain adequate records	Same as sole proprietorship	No	Same as sole proprietorship	Same as C corporation

9

Develop a Financial Strategy

Financial security is both a goal and a measure of self-reliance. Oddly, though, many of us treat our financial status as a residual of all our work—what's left over from our income after we spend what we want or must, and scramble to save what we can. We may do a pretty good job of making individual financial decisions, but we have no cohesive strategy to achieve financial security.

One reason for this lack of planning is the belief that we face too much uncertainty to plan, that we must simply do the best we can as situations develop and change. Another reason is that we don't have the knowledge to do financial planning. Neither of these reasons can be allowed to stand if you are truly to manage your personal enterprise. Uncertainty is precisely why you need to plan, and you can gain or hire the knowledge you need to do the job.

Libraries, bookstores, radio, television, and newspaper and magazine racks all carry information about financial planning.* Your advisers and specialized financial planners can help. Invest in your personal enterprise by learning at least the fundamentals.

---

* This chapter draws heavily on *Personal Financial Planning* by Hallman and Rosenbloom, McGraw-Hill.

ACTION STEP 84   *Set Financial Objectives and Strategies for Your Personal Enterprise*

You need clear objectives in order to develop strategies. Setting objectives will give you the structure of your financial plan and will help you learn some of the key factors involved. Here are the objectives we will examine:

1. Income
2. Protection from loss
3. Accumulation of wealth
4. Retirement planning
5. Tax and estate planning

ACTION STEP 85   *Set Your Income Objective*

Objectives for income may occasionally be as simple as "I want to make a million dollars before I'm forty." More often, income objectives should be a blend of desire, obligation, and reality. Too often the status quo is mistaken for reality and people set no objective at all.

The strategies available to you to achieve an income objective range from changing your job to upgrading your skills to changing your career to working more or working less, and so on. Earlier chapters in this book have stressed your responsibility to develop and promote the economic engine we are calling your personal enterprise.

The benefit of setting an income objective is that it makes you explicitly integrate your values. Time, effort, family, materialism, security, generosity, comfort, status, and achievement are some of the key values which get integrated into a number.

You can start to set your income objective by listing your obligations. Many reading this book who are in the baby boom generation face a triple whammy of *tuition, elder care,* and *saving for retirement*.

You may be able to reduce these needs or, through some means like bankruptcy, eliminate them. If you are in trouble with your obligations, you can consult with the Consumer Credit Counseling Service (1-800-388-2227), which has over 700 offices. For little or no fee, counselors will help you develop a plan to deal with your debts.

Age may bring you more or fewer obligations. Add to these things you need the things you want, in some order of priority and time.

Some difficulties in setting an income objective come from the need to know about other elements of your financial strategy, such as how insurance can be used and what it takes to retire comfortably. These difficulties are easily resolved by doing a complete plan and linking the elements together.

Another difficulty comes from the notion that once you define your income goal, you limit it. The fact is you have a much better chance of reaching a defined goal than no goal at all and, anyway, your income goal, like your whole financial strategy, should be a living document. Windfalls, setbacks, opportunities, problems, changes in obligations and values, and other factors that will affect your income objective are bound to occur. The great benefit of having a defined objective and strategy is that you can evaluate how these factors affect you, and can exert initiative to manage them. Your alternative is to react to each new event as it occurs and suffer the frustration and worry that comes from haste and lack of control.

ACTION STEP 86   *Protect Yourself from Loss*

Having in-demand skills and recognition from those who can pay for them may be the best insurance you can have, but it is not the only insurance you need. Illness, disability, death, property loss and liability, and unemployment all pose different needs for protection and deserve consideration for insurance, which you can either purchase or create.

Illness.   Medical insurance has become a central issue in our country. Spiraling costs, declining access, and the growing number of people with no coverage at all are causing the health care industry, politicians, and others to generate dozens of competing ideas about how to deal with the problem.

At this writing, it seems unlikely that Congress will adopt national medical insurance programs beyond Medicare, a federal health insurance program for people 65 and older and certain disabled people, and Medicaid, a federally mandated but state-structured set of programs primarily for low-income people.

A combination of private insurance, incentives, or mandates for business, and government "last resort" coverage will be combined with directives to further develop managed-care programs such as health maintenance organizations (HMOs), preferred provider organizations (PPOs), and other health care networks. Several states are experimenting with so-called guaranteed access plans. These plans tend to shift, not reduce, costs and the funding for them is not well defined.

Once again you have the obligation to stay current on events that affect your personal enterprise.

Your Rights under COBRA.   One big risk is losing your coverage because you lose your job. Another risk is needing coverage if you have a preexisting illness or injury. If you are employed and covered, you may already have a safety net. The COBRA Act of 1986 provides that if you work for a firm with more than 20 employees, you can keep your medical coverage for 18 months. (Some states are passing "little COBRA" acts which require similar extensions of coverage to employers with fewer than 20 employees.) Although you have to pay for the coverage, it is the same coverage and rate that your company had. When the COBRA coverage runs out you can, in most states, convert to a personal plan without a physical examination. The problem is that these plans typically don't offer the same level of benefits and are more costly than company plans.

If you are still being treated for a preexisting condition when your extension expires, you can get a conversion policy by being placed in a Health Reinsurance Association high-risk pool, but the premiums are very high. In Connecticut, a couple age 45 with children would pay over $1400 *per month* for a $500 deductible plan!

If you think your future might include self-employment, unemployment, or job changes, you might want to investigate a personal medical insurance policy. With a $1000 deductible,* a family policy might cost about $350 per month.

Get expert advice when buying any insurance, including medical insurance. Some individuals have found themselves in plans which

---

* As a rule, higher deductibles and lower premiums are desirable. A potential exception occurs when you are buying insurance as a corporation. See your accountant.

raise rates rapidly. That drives out those who are healthy and who can find other coverage, leaving fewer and fewer people remaining to pay more and more until the plan folds.

If you do cover yourself well and you become employed, try keeping your coverage and bargain with your employer to give you cash instead of its coverage. Many employers will willingly let you cover yourself and pay you to do it. Such a move frees them of both present and future liabilities. This strategy also protects you in the event the employer reduces or eliminates coverage.

Before you do find yourself uncovered, find out whether your state has emergency coverage, risk pools, or some other way for you to get covered. Learn whether insurers in your state have open enrollment. Based on the answers, you may want to buy and hold your own policy now, while you are in good health. A policy which has you pay most small claims but provides coverage for catastrophic illnesses may be enough for you.

A growing way to get certain kinds of coverage is the Employee Assistance Plan, or EAP. Originally set up by employers to provide counseling for alcoholism, these company-provided plans have evolved to provide counseling in a wide variety of areas from depression to grief to financial planning.

If you do cover yourself well and you become employed, try keeping your coverage and bargain with your employer to give you cash instead of its coverage.

No matter how you provide for your medical coverage, look ahead to see how you will be covered in retirement. Studies show that the last year of a person's life can often consume enormous medical expenses. Companies and insurers recognize that retirement benefits can drain a plan, and many are revising or even eliminating their programs. Generally, coverage in retirement isn't a problem. Medicare covers most major bills, and supplemental policies (often called *medigap* plans) are readily available. There are 10 standard (A through J) medigap plans, and prices can range from $10 per month to nearly $200, depending on benefits and your location.

If you plan any change in employment or a change to self-employment, make health insurance part of your plan. Being uninsured can bankrupt your personal enterprise and restrict, or even prohibit, access to treatment for you and your family.

Disability.   A disabling injury or illness can end your self-reliance and leave you at the mercy of others' generosity and the governments' vagaries. Disability is the biggest financial risk you face. In fact, the biggest cause of home mortgage foreclosures is disability.

If you are employed, you have safety nets. Workers' compensation laws, which vary by state, provide coverage for work-related injuries and illnesses. Some companies provide disability insurance as part of their package of benefits. Social security has a disability provision that becomes effective after a five-month waiting period. Payments will vary in amount depending on the amount of your wages subject to social security taxes.

However, most office workers don't become disabled under workers' compensation eligibility. Group disability often has severe limits on benefits, and social security pays only if you are totally unable to work.

Your objective here is to minimize the risk to your personal enterprise by having enough income to be self-sufficient should you become disabled. Simple budget analysis can show you how much you need, and some research on your employer's plan and on your social security entitlement will show you the coverage you have now. If there is a gap between your needs and the coverage, or if you face unemployment or self-employment, investigate a personal disability policy. A forty-year-old in reasonable health can get $3000 per month coverage for about $150 per month. Once again, you may want to have your own policy and bargain with your employer for cash instead of its coverage, but disability insurance is often an integral part of a group insurance plan.

Insurance advisers say that the most valuable asset you (and your personal enterprise) have is your future earnings. Protection from the loss of that asset by disability must be part of your plan.

Death.   Life insurance is a well-accepted way to protect those you care for from the loss caused by your premature death. The first variable in protecting from this loss is the amount of the loss you want to insure. Skilled agents can develop forecasts of the financial needs of those who depend on you, but you may decide to provide them with more or less than that estimate, and you may decide to vary that amount over time. The amount and timing of the coverage becomes your objective.

The second variable is the method you choose to provide the coverage. New insurance policies—they are more correctly called *products* now—are being developed all the time. Some are bare-bones term insurance and others are more like complex investment vehicles. *Time* is the key consideration in choosing the product, as life insurance is priced according to how long you wish to keep the death benefit in force. If you know you will be canceling your policy in five years or less, low-cost term insurance is appropriate. If you know you want to keep the policy for 10 years or more, an adjustable, universal, or whole life policy will be best.

If you have accumulated some wealth, you may also choose to provide a portion of the coverage for protection against this loss through your estate plan. Your choices about how to provide the coverage are your strategy.

Most people have, or at least know about, life insurance (see Figure 9-1), but many rely on company group policies for the bulk of their coverage. In today's world of cutbacks and job mobility that strategy may be faulty. Even if you keep your job, your company may redesign its insurance coverage. Test your strategy against the possible loss of your company coverage. If the impact of insufficient coverage is great, investigate a personal policy or product.

The three well-known insurance rating firms use these as their top two ratings:

A. M. Best	A++ and A+
Standard & Poors	AAA and AA+
Moody's	Aaa and Aa1

Of the approximately 2600 companies writing insurance, only about 20 have one of the top two ratings from all three rating firms.

You can confirm a company's rating by contacting your state insurance commissioner's office.

Figure 9-1. Insurance company ratings.

Property Loss and Liability.   Fire, theft, auto accident, and liability for your negligence are examples of potential losses which can threaten your personal enterprise. Your objective is to evaluate your exposure to these kinds of losses and decide the amount of coverage you need. Skilled insurance agents can provide you with information and techniques to do your evaluation.

Your strategy here will require a blend of insurance coverage and loss prevention, as well as a link with your legal strategy. Insurance products are available for all these risks, but their cost often depends on your degree of risk. Installation of an approved fire alarm system can reduce the cost of fire insurance. Driving fewer miles and maintaining a good driving record reduces auto insurance rates. You can directly lower your risks by following safety rules such as those relating to the storage of hazardous materials, installing effective locks, and driving safely.

Earlier in this section we discussed your legal strategy and suggested that you assess your liability exposure. Your liability from injuring someone in a car accident or from someone slipping on your steps is best handled by auto or home owners' insurance. Your liability from service on a board of directors or even a voluntary town commission, however, requires specific coverage. The company or town may provide partial or complete coverage, but you may decide that the risk is too high. Your strategy will be to either secure additional coverage or to resign and eliminate the risk.

Unemployment.   Protecting against this final loss through self-reliance has been the subject of much of this book. But even the best strategies for self-reliance can encounter disasters such as injury, illness, company shutdowns, and so on. The good news is that you do have spending and saving choices you can make to limit your risk.

Spending choices to stay within your means are obviously desirable, but what may be more important is the level of committed spending which you have. People often refer to their monthly "nut" when they talk about the payments they are required to make. If you are concerned about an unemployment risk, keep this amount low. If it's too high now, take action to get it restructured or reduced. Bankers and others are more willing to talk about refinancing and spreading payments with people who are employed. Selling assets such as second homes, boats, and so on is easier to do when you are not under pressure of foreclosure.

Saving, or having wealth in some form, is the only real way to be protected from the loss of unemployment. Some ideas about accumulating wealth will be presented later in this chapter.

Don't wait to find out how you'll make out financially if you lose a job. If you have a budget, review it. After you build your budget based on today's income, build a "doomsday budget" based on losing your income. Most people find this hard to do. It takes more than cutting out luxuries like vacations and dining out; it means getting extra wear out of old clothes, selling unneeded items—perhaps a second car—finding cheaper food items, or even down-scaling your housing.

> *Self-reliance means you provide for savings and other protection out of your present income before any discretionary spending.*

Make bold cuts in this budget. A big mistake is to nibble at these cutbacks, cutting a little this month and a little more next month, slowly sliding into debt, or worse. If you do lose your job, *make your cuts fast and deep.* You'll conserve more money faster and you won't have to spend hours on every decision to spend money. If it's not in the budget, it doesn't get spent.

Tell people. If your income stops, you need the cooperation of your creditors. Visit your bank or mortgage holder. Request postponement of payments or partial payments. If you have a VA or FHA mortgage, ask about forbearance, an emergency relief program to avoid foreclosure. If you rent, tell your landlord. Perhaps you can exchange work for rent.

Notify your other creditors, especially your utilities. Propose a partial payment program and commit to keeping them informed.

Learn what government offers. Unemployment compensation is the most well-known program to help those who lose their jobs. These state-run programs vary by state, but are similar enough to use Connecticut as an example.

The minimum weekly benefit rate is $15 and the most recent maximum is $270. The rate is based on earnings in a base period—a 12-month period (4 calendar quarters)—from which wages are used to calculate entitlement.

In Connecticut, the weekly benefit rate is determined by dividing the high quarter of earnings by the number 26. The number arrived at is then rounded to the next-lower dollar. The minimum benefit rate is $15 and the current maximum is $270, effective October 7, 1990.

> *Example:* (High-quarter earnings) $3973.68 divided by 26
>   = $152.84 (rounded to) $152.

To determine if a person has sufficient wage credits to establish a benefit year, the law requires that he or she must have a total amount of base-period earnings that equals or exceeds 40 times the weekly benefit rate. If we used the weekly benefit rate of $152 contained in the preceding example, it would have been necessary for this individual to have earned total base-period wages of $6080 or more to qualify.

Maximum benefits represents the total amount of benefits that can be paid in the benefit year. The law provides that the maximum amount payable is computed by multiplying the weekly benefit rate times the number 26. Using the $152 weekly benefit rate in the earlier example, the maximum benefits for that individual would be $3952. This figure does not include dependency.

> *Example:* (Weekly benefit rate) $152 \times 26 = $3952.

Number of weeks, maximum, of regular benefits payable is normally 26. An individual who collects partial unemployment (special rules) or who has a pension (special rules) may receive benefits for more than 26 weeks, but is still limited to the same maximum benefits (26 times the weekly benefit rate).

You may be eligible for a dependency allowance of $10 weekly for each child for whom you are the whole or main support and who falls into one of the following categories:

1. Under 18 years of age
2. Under 21 years of age and a full-time student
3. A mentally or physically handicapped child of any age

Total dependency allowances cannot be paid for more than five dependents ($50) and may never exceed half your weekly benefit rate.

Waiting times to begin benefits vary, depending on whether your unemployment was voluntary or not. If it was not, waiting time is

only a week or two. If you left your job on your own, you should consult the rules for your state.

Learn now. Find out now which government agencies and programs might help you. These include Medicaid, aid to dependent
children, food stamps, state health services, veterans benefits, social
security programs, and more. Your United Way can give you information.

ACTION STEP 87   *Plan for Your Accumulation of Wealth*

Your wealth might come from inheritance, the increased value of
your business or investments, gifts, pension distribution, or some
windfall, but most likely it will start with the excess of your income
over your spending. Your objectives and strategies for accumulating
wealth will be strongly influenced by your tax status.

---

*Wealth is the value of what you own. The stream of income you earn
isn't wealth until it gets converted to something of value.*

Setting an objective for the accumulation of wealth is similar to
setting an objective for income. On the surface, it may seem futile
and best served by simply being opportunistic, but the same impera-
tive applies: you have a much better chance of achieving a clear
objective than none at all.

Here is a frame of reference for building the wealth it might take
to send a child to college. Assume you save $3000 per year and invest
it at 7 percent compounded. In 5 years, you would have $21,460; in
10 years you would have $47,351; and in 15 years the total would be
$66,412.

How to build wealth is a broad field of its own. Wealth is not to be
confused with income. Wealth is the value of what you own. The
stream of income you earn isn't wealth until it gets converted to
something of value.

Your savings, stocks, and other securities, antiques, jewelry, and
the equity in your home are examples of things of value, and they are
the safety stock in your personal enterprise.

You can convert income into wealth by following a conservative strategy of saving and investing or a high risk-high reward strategy of leveraged options, real estate speculation, and the like. Bookshelves are full of books on how to invest. Investment counselors are readily available, and we have covered the process of evaluating advisers. Our purpose here is to urge that you include a specific objective for accumulating wealth as a part of your financial strategy of self-reliance.

ACTION STEP 88   *Plan for Your Retirement*

Much the same can be said for this objective; written and professional advice is abundant, but many people don't take the initiative to set objectives and develop strategies.

The four elements of your retirement plan will be *your pension(s) and retirement accounts, your social security benefits, your insurance programs,* and *your wealth.*

Your Pension(s).   A qualified pension from long service with a company is becoming a less frequent and less secure cornerstone of financial security in retirement. People change jobs more often, companies cease to exist, and pension plans fail. Legislation to create "portable pensions" with mandated minimum contributions by employers has been introduced, but passage does not appear likely.

Risky pensions coupled with rising health costs and dwindling government aid result in a potential crisis for those who fail to plan adequately for retirement.

Your pension(s) and retirement accounts from employers should be evaluated for value and safety. Get a copy of the plan and review it with your insurance agent and your accountant.

Pay particular attention to the early retirement options. Many companies are offering early retirement to employees as a way to cut payroll. Be sure you understand what, if any, penalties you will suffer in your payout.

You can make projections to estimate the value (payout) of the plan as it's written. A *defined contribution* plan places the risk level of the ultimate benefit on the employee, whereas a *defined benefit* plan places the burden of meeting a specified benefit level on the employer. If the value of the plan is insufficient for your retirement, or if you believe you may not acquire enough benefits under the plan because of job mobility or some other reason, you may want to establish an individual retirement program. One type, the 401k (403b for government and nonprofit organizations) plans are employer-sponsored tax deferred retirement accounts. Employees can contribute a percentage of their pay (currently up to $8728) to their own account, often matched by the employer. Other, nonemployer retirement plans are mentioned later.

The security of your plan is more difficult to evaluate. The Employee Retirement Income Security Act (ERISA) regulates and protects pension and other benefit programs and payments, but its four titles are subject to extremely complex exceptions.

The first question to answer is whether your plan is adequately funded. Ask the plan administrator or your advisors to show you how the benefits are being provided. If there is an adequate fund of invested capital, you are more secure than if benefits are being paid fully or in part from current operations, which could fail.

A funded plan is no guarantee of security these days. If the fund is backed by guaranteed investment contracts (GICs) from an insurer, evaluate the insurer. Many, including some big names like Mutual Benefit Life, have become insolvent and left contract holders and beneficiaries at risk. (See Figure 9-1.)

You can choose how your 401k funds are invested. In addition to GICs, the choices most often include stock funds (for those seeking faster appreciation) and bond funds (for those seeking more security).

Because situations change, you should not risk your self-reliance in retirement by relying solely on employer pensions.

Your Social Security.   The basic concept of social security is that, during one's working years, employees, employers, and self-employed individuals pay social security taxes (FICA taxes), which are pooled in special trust funds. Then, when a covered worker retires, dies, or becomes totally disabled, monthly benefits are paid to the worker and/or his or her dependents to replace part of the earnings lost as a result of these events or risks.

Part of the contributions to social security goes into a separate Hospital Insurance Trust Fund so that when workers and their dependents reach age 65 they will have coverage (Medicare) for their hospital bills.

How Your Benefit Is Figured.   In general, a social security benefit is based on your earnings, averaged over most of your working lifetime. This is different from many private pension plans that are usually based on a relatively small number of years of earnings.

In its simplest terms, here's how your social security benefit is figured according to a government pamphlet.

Step 1   We determine the number of years of earnings to use as a base.

     Retirement benefits: For everybody born after 1928 and retiring in 1991 or later, which includes most people reading this booklet, that number is 35 years. Fewer years are used for people born in 1928 or earlier.

     Disability and survivors benefits: We use most of the years of earnings posted to your record.

Step 2   We adjust these earnings for inflation.

Step 3   We determine your *average* adjusted earnings based on the number of years figured in step 1.

Step 4   We multiply your average adjusted earnings by percentages in a formula that is specified by law.

     That formula results in benefits that replace about 42 percent of a person's earnings. This applies to people who had *average* earnings during their working years. The percentage is lower for people in the upper-income brackets, and higher for people with low incomes. (That's because the social security benefit formula is weighted in favor of low-income workers who have less opportunity to save and invest during their working years.)

You can find out your projected income from social security by calling (800) 234-5772. Be sure you understand the assumptions of your earnings that go into the projection.

Your Insurance Programs.   You may have purchased insurance policies having features which can provide money in retirement. Paid-up policies or policies with cash values can be converted to income streams or, in some cases, redeemed for a lump sum. Your financial strategy needs to integrate your retirement objectives with those objectives you have already developed (as discussed previously) for protection from loss.

Annuity products are intended to provide a stream of payments. *Immediate annuities* are those which are purchased for a lump sum and which then provide a stream of income that is guaranteed for life. *Deferred annuities* are those which are purchased over time as a form of retirement savings. The growth of those retirement savings is tax-deferred.

Your age is a major consideration in selecting an insurance component in your retirement strategy. The complexity of the products and the actuarial factors which affect price and benefits make it important that you get good advice.

Your Wealth.   If you are like most people, you will have to save and invest to build wealth for some portion of your retirement and, like most people, you may be shocked at what it will take. The exercises following will give you an idea of what you will need and what you will have to put aside to reach your goal.

Thinking about saving 15, 18, or 73 percent of your gross pay may come as a shock, but your self-reliance depends on knowing these facts.

Other factors you should consider are how much income your retirement nest egg will produce and how long it will last. Figure 9-2 lets you calculate both factors.

Retirement Planning Exercises

All examples assume social security benefits—these are additional amounts needed to achieve the income goals.

Your goal is to provide adequate income that will adjust for inflation, and that hopefully you will not outlive, after you have suffered a *100 percent loss of wages*—which is the reality of retirement.

How to Estimate Your Needs

A detailed plan requires a thorough knowledge of:

- Tax laws
- Investments and markets
- Your income and future prospects
- Your investment risk propensity and assumptions concerning:

inflation rates before and after retirement

planned retirement age

income goals

life expectancy

growth rate of your income

social security benefits

pension plan benefit limits

If you have sufficient knowledge about all these elements and are computer literate, there are some retail software programs available to play with, but none will be recommended here.

A better course of action is to have a report prepared by someone with expert knowledge in this field. A financial planner or accountant who provides financial planning services should charge about $250. A commission-based financial professional, such as a career life insurance agent and some stockbrokers, will often provide this type of report at no cost.

Figure 9-2 and the three examples which follow can help you approximate your situation, but should not be used to make any decisions.

The villain in retirement planning is inflation. The past generation's average wage can be the next generation's poverty level.

How Much Income Will Your "Nest Egg" Produce?

1. Amount currently in retirement fund
   (income-producing assets)   _____

2. Annual income needed to live desired lifestyle   _____

3. Less fixed sources of annual retirement income:
   Pension   _____   _____
   Social security   _____
   Other_____   _____

4. Balance which must come from "nest egg"   _____

5. Withdrawal from "nest egg" as a percentage of the entire fund
   _____ divided by _____ equals _____%

6. Assumed average rate of return on the fund   _____%

How Long Will the "Nest Egg" Last?

% on Line 5	5	6	7	8	9	10	11	12	13	14	15	16
40	3	3	3	3	3	3	3	3	3	3	3	3
35	3	3	3	3	3	4	4	4	4	4	4	4
30	4	4	4	4	4	4	4	5	5	5	5	5
25	5	5	5	5	5	5	6	6	6	6	7	7
24	5	5	5	5	5	6	6	6	6	7	7	7
23	5	5	5	6	6	6	6	7	7	7	8	8
22	5	5	6	6	6	6	7	7	7	8	8	8
21	6	6	6	6	6	7	7	7	8	8	9	10
20	6	6	6	7	7	7	8	8	9	9	10	11
19	6	7	7	7	7	8	8	9	9	10	11	12
18	7	7	7	8	8	9	9	10	10	11	13	15
17	7	7	8	8	9	9	10	11	12	13	15	19
16	8	8	9	9	10	10	11	12	14	16	20	
15	8	9	9	10	11	12	13	14	16	21		
14	9	10	10	11	12	13	15	17	22			
13	10	11	11	12	14	15	18	23				
12	11	12	13	14	16	19	24					
11	12	14	15	17	20	25						
10	14	16	18	21	27							
9	17	19	22	29								
8	20	24	31									
7	26	33										

Percentage rate of return on investment (Line 6)

The place where the two columns intersect indicates the number of years the fund will last.

(The fund would not be consumed in this lower area because the annual rate of return exceeds the annual rate of withdrawal.)

Figure 9-2. Factors to consider in retirement planning.

Exercises

1. A 35-year-old woman earning $40,000 per year, with no assets accumulated, wishes to retire at age 67 with $4000 per month in today's purchasing power.

   Inflation is 4 percent per year and her earning will increase 7 percent per year. Assuming she lives 20 years beyond retirement, the amount she needs to have accumulated at retirement is $1,715,416.

   Using a tax-deferred plan that earns 8 percent a year, she would have to save 15.6 percent of her salary. Today, that would be $520 per month, but the amount would increase 7 percent per year along with her salary.

2. A 45-year-old man earning $75,000 a year, with accumulated assets of $10,000, wishes to retire at age 66 with $5000 per month in today's purchasing power.

   Inflation is 4 percent and his earnings will increase 4 percent per year. Assuming he lives 20 years beyond retirement and that his assets have grown to $250,000, the added amount he needs to have accumulated at retirement is $832,988.

   Using a tax-deferred plan that earns 8 percent a year, he would have to save 18 percent of his salary. Today, that would be $1123 per month, but the amount would increase 4 percent per year along with his salary.

3. A 55-year-old man earning $100,000 a year, with accumulated assets of $80,000, wishes to retire at age 65 with $6666 per month in today's purchasing power.

   Inflation is 4 percent and his earnings will increase 4 percent per year. Assuming he lives 20 years beyond retirement and that his assets have grown to $170,000, the added amount he needs to have accumulated at retirement is $1,197,527.

   Using a tax-deferred plan that earns 8 percent a year, he would have to save *73.3* percent of his salary. Today, that would be $6108 per month, but the amount would increase 4 percent per year along with his salary.

Individual Retirement Accounts (IRAs) and Company Plans.

As an individual or company owner, you may be able to create retirement programs which, under some conditions, let you defer taxes on the contribution and the interest earned on those contributions. IRAs are intended to permit employed people who have no company-provided pension plan to establish a retirement fund. The maximum allowed for deductions is $2000. If the spouse works and also has no qualified pension coverage from an employer, both can contribute $2000 as deductible contributions. If the spouse does not work, $250 is the allowed amount. More can be contributed, but no added deduction from gross income is allowed.

If you have a corporation, you can adopt a qualified pension plan. Some are complex and expensive to administer, but one type is not. A Simplified Employee Pension (SEP-IRA) lets you deduct and deposit 15 percent of compensation up to $30,000. There are no setup costs and no reporting requirements. Contributions are flexible from 0 to 15 percent and you can exclude any employees for three years. The only form you need to keep on file is free from the IRS.

An example of the power of using a plan to contribute pretax money versus after-tax money can be seen in the following table. Assume a 45-year-old contributes $2000 per year until age 65:

	Without plan	With plan	
Contribution	$2000	$2000	
Taxes @33%	660	0	
Net after-tax contribution	1340	2000	
After-tax accumulation at age 65 Contributions compounded:			
			Advantage with plan
@5% per year	$40,341	$46,524	15%
@8% per year	$52,250	$66,227	27%
@10% per year	$56,729	$84,423	49%

Other Wealth.   Your retirement strategy can include liquidation of your wealth. Stocks, bonds, partnership or other business interests, and personal property can be converted to cash. A growing method of converting wealth to cash is the reverse equity mortgage loan. The older homeowner can borrow on the equity in the home. The loan can be provided in a lump payment, payments for life, payments for a specified number of years, or just a line of credit. The federal government requires counseling for those seeking reverse equity mortgages which are to have federal guarantees.

Counseling is important for any retirement strategy which includes wealth liquidation. The obvious risk is that you will outlive the value of your assets and be left destitute unless you have other elements.

But a less obvious risk, and one which many retirees overlook, is the impact of inflation on retirement income. If you live for just 10 years after retirement and inflation averages only 4 percent, the purchasing power of your fixed income of today will be reduced by nearly *half*. If you live for 15 years, 80 percent of your income will be eaten by higher prices.

It would be a tragedy if you spent your working years building self-reliance only to lose it to inflation.

ACTION STEP 89   *Conduct Tax and Estate Planning*

These two technical and very individualized strategies are beyond the scope of this book, but three examples are included here to show you how important it is for you to develop your objectives and to plan for them.

1. *Medicaid Planning.*   Should you have concerns about becoming destitute, or should your other financial planning reveal that you may somehow become a Medicaid recipient, you need to do Medicaid planning. You'll recall that Medicaid is the medical insurance provided by states in cooperation with the federal government and intended for those who cannot pay.

The objective of this controversial type of planning is to shift assets, divert income, and structure your finances so that you can qualify for Medicaid coverage without leaving you or your spouse bankrupt. The classic, often-told case involves a couple who lives in a rented apartment but owns a $200,000 vacation home. They have some savings and a small, but adequate, income. The husband becomes ill and enters a nursing home. He gets no Medicaid coverage until he exhausts the $200,000 because the vacation home is "countable" as wealth because it's not the couple's prime dwelling. In this case, a change of residence might have protected the asset.

Medicaid was created for the "impoverished" and the definition of what constitutes poverty is not fixed. Basically, what happens is that a "snapshot" is taken of the combined assets of the husband and wife. The couple must *spend down* assets to the poverty level. "Not countable" in that snapshot are the primary home, one car, such personal items as wedding rings, some life insurance, and the *spouse's own income.*

If you are thinking about planning for Medicaid, be aware that property transfers must take place 30 months before application for benefits, and under some conditions the recapture period may be 60 months.

The rules about what are "countable" and "noncountable" assets, and the tactics available to you, are complex enough to warrant a separate planning session with your advisors.

2. *Distribution of the Assets in Your Estate.* To have your assets distributed in the manner you set forth in your will, they must go through the probate process. Be aware that many of your assets will pass to others through ownership designations such as "joint and survivor" on property and bank accounts. Others pass by beneficiary designation, such as with life insurance, pensions, and IRA accounts. None of these is governed by your will. Be certain that your estate planning team is aware of all these assets in order to help you achieve your goals for distribution.

3. *Trusts, Gifts, and Tax Planning.* Accumulated assets in people's estates are subject to attachment during life to pay for medical and nursing home care and decimation from estate taxes after death. Planning can allow you to maintain the income from and the use of your assets while sheltering them from those risks, but these actions must be taken in advance of illness or death to be effective. Consult your estate planning team.

10

Develop a Personal Wellness Strategy

The risk in writing about a "personal enterprise" is that readers might focus too much on the "enterprise." We have used terms like *investment, promotion, strategy,* and other business analogies to make points about building self-reliance. The risk is that you might neglect the "personal."

> *Your* personal *enterprise is built on one and only one foundation— you.*

You can take the initiative to protect yourself and enhance your wellness by *guarding your safety, practicing prevention, exercising, choosing what you eat and drink,* and *putting balance in your life.*

ACTION STEP 90   *Guard Your Personal Safety*

Accidents and fire claim over 100,000 lives a year in the United States. Auto accidents are the single biggest factor, and all parties— auto makers, insurers, health care providers, and safety experts— agree that using seat belts and having air bags saves lives and reduces accident severity. Unfortunately, hospital emergency rooms still see that *half* of all crash victims suffer more death and injury because they found seat belts too uncomfortable.

Emergency rooms also see crash victims who had too much to drink. Traffic crashes are the leading cause of death in the United

States for all age groups from 1 through 34, and almost half of these fatalities are alcohol related.

Fire safety in offices and homes involves eliminating hazards, having extinguishers, and installing and maintaining alarms.

These admonitions about safety, drinking, and fire may sound like clichés, but more than 100,000 lives a year in the United States could be saved and several hundred thousand serious injuries could be avoided if they were followed. What makes these admonitions so worthwhile is that you can follow all of them if you simply: *Buckle your seat belt, don't have that drink, and put a fresh battery in your smoke alarm.*

ACTION STEP 91   *Practice Preventive Health Care*

The facts on preventive health care are growing.

- We know now that smoking is a hazard.
- We know that immunizations are beneficial.
- Preventive dental care is a fully accepted practice.
- We have learned that high blood pressure, excessive cholesterol, glaucoma, diabetes, breast cancer, osteoporosis, prostate cancer, stress, and a host of other illnesses can be caught through screenings and tests.

Unfortunately, the United States lags the world in preventive medicine. We don't immunize children at an early age—only Haiti and Bolivia have lower immunization rates for children under two years old.

Our health care system typically does not pay for such things as a $400 osteoporosis test or $1000 prenatal care—yet we will not hesitate to pay $15,000 for a broken hip or $25,000 to $50,000 to keep a low-weight baby in an intensive care nursery.

Not everyone needs or should have every screening medical science can provide. Your doctor and your hospital can best advise you. One popular tool today is called a *Health Risk Assessment* (HRA), which uses one or several extensive questionnaires about your health history and habits in conjunction with the evaluation of a health professional to assess your risk for certain diseases.

A general HRA, "The Health Test" from National Health Enhancement Systems, is reprinted as Appendix B.

ACTION STEP 92   *Get Exercise and Rest*

Staying in demand takes stamina. Regular exercise and adequate rest earn you high stamina that can power you through tough work loads. They also contribute to improved muscle tone and stronger cardiovascular (heart) and pulmonary (lung) functioning.

Exercise can reduce stress and build self-esteem. Over time, as it builds your stamina and helps make your sleep more sound, it can reduce fatigue.

Americans seem schizophrenic about exercise. Some are obsessive (though perhaps episodic), and others do not exercise at all. We Americans have a set of standards about our self-image. We see that slim, vigorous image in all our advertising and entertainment. Yet, our children are failing basic fitness tests and we are the most obese nation on earth.

ACTION STEP 93   *Choose What You Eat and Drink*

Nutrition is fast expanding its significance from being simply a major contributor to weight management and general well-being. Today, what and how much we eat is seen as critical in affecting the incidence and management of specific diseases, such as heart disease and cancer.

Knowing that fruits, vegetables, and grains are good for you and that drugs, alcohol, fat, salt, and sugar are not isn't enough. Good nutrition must be first your choice and then your habit.

Here are three clinically sound books on nutrition:

1. *Modern Nutrition in Health and Disease* by Maurice Shils, M.D., Sc.D. (Lea & Febiger, 1988).
2. *Basic Nutrition and Diet Therapy* by Sue Rodwell Williams (9th ed. Mosby Yearbook, 1992).
3. *Nutrition for Living* by Janet Christian and Janet Greger (Benjamin/Cummings, 1991).

ACTION STEP 94   *Put Some Balance in Your Life*

Reading on a wide range of subjects, spending time with family and friends, traveling, and other experiences can prepare you to see new opportunities. Setting aside time to do things simply for enjoyment is both beneficial and rewarding.

Self-improvement books and seminars continue to be best-sellers as people search for ways to relieve their personal concerns and frustrations.

Recently, a wave of books and programs about stress reduction have hit the market. Stress is often caused by feelings of helplessness and frustration. The personal development program advocated in this book fights stress because it involves purposeful action that leads to control over your life.

Though a few have elevated wellness to an end in itself, your wellness strategy does have to be aggressive but does not have to be all-consuming.

Being an alert, well-informed, physically healthy person should be more than an attractive mental image—it should be your clear objective. All of the things we have talked about, all the strategies we have suggested, aren't only done *for* you, they are done *by* you. The better condition you are in, the better job you can do for yourself and the longer you can do it.

Conclusion

This book concludes, then, on the same theme with which it opened. You cannot rely for economic survival on other people, government, or the traditional employer-employee relationship. To stay in demand, you must treat yourself as your own personal enterprise; investing in yourself and promoting yourself to make job offers come to you.

The goal is self-reliance—and the one person who can provide it is you.

Appendix A
Self-Promotion Matrix

Targets	Techniques						
	SIPR	Meetings	Join organizations	Communication	Political activity	Charity	Get quoted
Your boss							
Other bosses							
Co-workers (past and present)							
Recruiters							
Employers in your industry							
Faculty members							
Employers in your area							
Public accountants and auditors							
Bankers							
Analysts, commentators							
Regulators							
Professional associates							
Civic club members							
Charitable organizations							
Alumni							
Friends							
Neighbors							
Classmates							
Media people							
Customers							
Suppliers							
Dentists and doctors							
Clergy							

					Techniques				
Write articles	Pro bono consulting	Lecture	Lead seminars	Teach courses	Conduct surveys	Gifts	Send articles	Publicity	Networking

Appendix B
The Health Test

*Take the first step to a healthier life!**

Are you facing risks that can affect your chances of living a long and healthy life? The Health Test can help you find out. Most important, this personalized evaluation can help you learn how to improve your health and well-being while you reduce your controllable long-term health risks. Prevention and early detection are the keys to maximizing your health potential. That's what The Health Test is all about.

It starts with this easy-to-complete, confidential questionnaire. Just print your name, address, and the necessary personal information at the top and start in. Most of your answers simply require you to check the appropriate response. A few will ask you to write in a specific number. When you've filled it out as accurately and honestly as possible, we'll have the information we need to complete your individual report.

Your personalized Health Test report will contain specific information about the way your lifestyle impacts your overall health outlook. You'll learn how you can change the way you live to increase your chances of remaining healthy and active as you grow older.

The Health Test only takes a few minutes. But those few minutes could change your life . . . perhaps even save your life. Please, take the first step toward healthier living right now.

IMPORTANT: The Health Test can't predict whether or not you might develop a particular type of disease. It's not a substitute for regular medical checkups, either. The Health Test is designed to screen healthy people with no indication of disease. If you already have a disease, this report and its recommendations may not be accurate or appropriate for you.

FOR OFFICE USE ONLY			
Org _____	Cla _____	Occ _____	Ins _____
Pro _____	Ret _____	Ref _____	Bat _____

The Health Test™ is a product of National Health Enhancement Systems,ˢᴹ providing health and fitness evaluations through a national network of selected healthcare institutions.

©National Health Enhancement Systems, Inc. 1991. Phoenix, Arizona.
7/91

* Reproduced by permission.

Please print clearly

Name _____

Address _____

City _____ State _____ Zip Code _____

Social Security # _____

Today's Date ___ / ___ / ___   Birthdate ___ / ___ / ___

Telephone (___) _____ (___) _____
                         Daytime   Evening

Type of health coverage: HMO _____ PPO _____ Major Medical _____
Medicare/Medicaid _____ None _____ Other _____

Name of Health Insurance Company (if any):

_____

The "age," "sex," "weight," "height," and "race" questions must be answered in order to accurately appraise your current health risk.

Age _____ Sex _____ Weight _____ lbs. Height _____ ft. _____ in.
Race _____   (1) Caucasian (2) Black (3) Hispanic (4) Oriental
              (5) American Indian (6) Other

1. Do you have parents, brothers, or sisters who have had a heart attack or heart by-pass surgery?
   ____ a. Yes, at age 59 or before
   ____ b. Yes, at age 60 or after
   ____ c. No, or don't know

2. Have you ever had any of the following conditions?
   (Check all that apply)
   ____ a. Heart Attack
   ____ b. Angina (diagnosed chest pain)
   ____ c. Heart By-pass Surgery
   ____ d. Angioplasty
   ____ e. Stroke
   ____ f. Blood Vessel Surgery
   ____ g. Diabetes—Beginning at what age? ____

3. How long has it been since your last complete medical examination?
   ____ a. ____ Years
   ____ b. Never or don't know   (99)

4. Do you currently have a physician with whom you can discuss the results of this test?
_____ a. Yes
_____ b. No

5. Do/did you smoke cigarettes?
_____ a. Yes, I do now
_____ b. Yes, but I have stopped
_____ c. No, I have never smoked (go to question 8)

6. What is/was the average number of cigarettes you smoke(d) each day?
_____ cigarettes

7. If you no longer smoke, how many years ago did you quit?
_____ years ago

8. Do you smoke a pipe or cigar?
_____ a. Yes
_____ b. No

9. Do you use smokeless tobacco (snuff or chewing tobacco)?
_____ a. Yes
_____ b. No

10. If you have had your blood pressure taken in the last year, was it:
_____ a. Elevated or high
_____ b. Borderline
_____ c. Normal or low
_____ d. Not taken or don't know blood pressure

11. If you know your blood pressure, please write it below.
a. Systolic (high number) _____
b. Diastolic (low number) _____

12. If you have had your serum cholesterol measured within the last year, was the value:
_____ a. Elevated or high
_____ b. About average
_____ c. Low
_____ d. Not measured or don't know cholesterol

13. If you know your serum cholesterol value, please write it below (e.g., 180, 210, etc.).
Cholesterol value _____

14. How often do you eat fatty cuts of meat such as beef steak, hamburger, sausage, bacon, and/or luncheon meats?
_____ a. Two or more times a day
_____ b. Daily
_____ c. 3–6 times a week
_____ d. Twice a week or less

15. How many eggs do you eat a week? (Include those used in cooking.)
_____ a. 7 or more
_____ b. 4–6
_____ c. 3 or less

16. How often do you drink WHOLE milk or have whole milk products (ice cream, butter, cheese, cream)?
_____ a. Two or more times a day
_____ b. Daily
_____ c. 3–6 times a week
_____ d. Twice a week or less

17. How often do you eat fried foods?
_____ a. Daily
_____ b. 3–6 times a week
_____ c. Twice a week or less

18. How often do you add cream sauces, creamy salad dressings, or gravy to your food?
_____ a. Two or more times a day
_____ b. Daily
_____ c. 3–6 times a week
_____ d. Twice a week or less

19. How often do you participate in vigorous endurance exercise such as brisk walking, running, swimming, cycling, or aerobic dancing for 15 to 30 minutes?
_____ a. 3 or more times a week
_____ b. 1 to 2 times a week
_____ c. Less than once a week

20. Do you participate in stretching exercises for muscle and joint flexibility at least three times a week?
_____ a. Yes
_____ b. No

21. Do you participate two or more times a week in strengthening or muscle toning exercises such as weight training or calisthenics?
_____ a. Yes
_____ b. No

22. How well do the following traits describe you: COMPETITIVE, BOSSY, EASILY ANGERED, PRESSED FOR TIME?
_____ a. Very well
_____ b. Fairly well
_____ c. Not at all

23. Is your energy level lower than it used to be?
_____ a. Yes
_____ b. No

24. Do you seem to worry about things more than other people?
_____ a. Yes
_____ b. No

25. Is your sense of satisfaction or pleasure in life as high as you would like it to be?
_____ a. Yes
_____ b. No

26. Do you easily become angry over small problems or disappointments at home or work?
_____ a. Yes
_____ b. No

27. Are you finding it difficult to get along with people, or are people having trouble getting along with you?
_____ a. Yes
_____ b. No

28. Do you drive a motor vehicle while under the influence of alcohol or other drugs?
_____ a. Yes
_____ b. No

29. Do you wear a seat belt while driving or riding in a motor vehicle?
_____ a. Never
_____ b. 25% of the time
_____ c. 50% of the time
_____ d. 75% of the time
_____ e. Always

30. Do you have smoke alarms in your home?
_____ a. Yes
_____ b. No

31. Do you keep a loaded gun in your home or motor vehicle?
_____ a. Yes
_____ b. No

32. Are all poisons, cleaning solvents, and other chemicals around your home clearly labeled and kept out of the reach of children?
_____ a. Yes
_____ b. No

33. Do you currently drink alcoholic beverages?
_____ a. Yes. If yes, enter the average number of drinks per week.
      Bottles of beer per week _____
      Glasses of wine per week _____
      Shots of liquor per week _____
_____ b. No

34. How often do you use non-prescribed drugs or medications which affect your mood or help you to relax (such as tranquilizers or stimulants)?
  ____ a. Almost every day
  ____ b. Sometimes
  ____ c. Rarely or never

35. Have you had any of the following problems recently which you have NOT discussed with a physician? (Check all that apply.)
  ____ a. Change in bowel or bladder habits
  ____ b. A sore that does not heal
  ____ c. Unusual bleeding or discharge
  ____ d. Thickening or lump in the breast or elsewhere
  ____ e. Indigestion or difficulty in swallowing
  ____ f. An obvious change in a wart or mole
  ____ g. A nagging cough or hoarseness

36. When in the sun for an hour or more, do you wear protective clothing or use a sun screen?
  ____ a. Yes
  ____ b. No

37. How often do you have rectal and colon exams?
  ____ a. At least once per year
  ____ b. Once every 3 years
  ____ c. More than 3 years apart
  ____ d. Never

FOR MEN ONLY

38. How often do you have prostate exams?
  ____ a. At least once per year
  ____ b. Once every 3 years
  ____ c. More than 3 years apart
  ____ d. Never

FOR WOMEN ONLY

39. How often do you examine your breasts for lumps?
  ____ a. Monthly
  ____ b. Once every few months
  ____ c. Rarely or never

40. How often do you have a Pap Test performed?
  ____ a. At least once per year
  ____ b. Once every 3 years
  ____ c. More than 3 years apart
  ____ d. Never

AREAS OF SPECIAL INTEREST

Check which of the following health areas would be of interest to you or your spouse.   (S-B)

		Self	Spouse	
41.	Family Doctor or Specialist	_____	_____	41.
42.	Comprehensive Medical Checkup	_____	_____	42.
43.	Comprehensive Cardiovascular Evaluation	_____	_____	43.
44.	Blood Pressure/Cholesterol Check	_____	_____	44.
45.	Reducing Risk of Heart Attack/Stroke	_____	_____	45.
46.	Weight Management Program	_____	_____	46.
47.	Stress Management Program	_____	_____	47.
48.	Cancer Risk Reduction Program	_____	_____	48.
49.	Stop Smoking/Tobacco Stoppers Program	_____	_____	49.
50.	Seniors' Programs	_____	_____	50.
51.	Women's Health Programs	_____	_____	51.
52.	Low Back Care	_____	_____	52.
53.	Fitness Assessment/Custom Exercise Program	_____	_____	53.
54.	Exercise/Aerobic Program	_____	_____	54.
55.	Sports Medicine	_____	_____	55.

Questions 56 and 57 are optional and are used as statistical data only:

56. Total yearly household income
   _____ a. Less than $15,000
   _____ b. $15,000–24,999
   _____ c. $25,000–34,999
   _____ d. $35,000–44,999
   _____ e. $45,000–54,999
   _____ f. More than $55,000

57. Highest level of education completed
   _____ a. High School
   _____ b. Some College
   _____ c. College
   _____ d. Graduate School
   _____ e. None of the above

To be completed by a physician or health professional (Optional).

58. Height _____ in.

59. Weight _____ lbs.

60. Blood Pressure _____ / _____ mmHg

61. Body Fat ____ %
      Sum 3 Site ____ mm
      Sum 7 Site ____ mm
62. Total Cholesterol ____ mg/dl
63. HDL Cholesterol ____ mg/dl
64. Triglycerides ____ mg/dl
65. LDL Cholesterol ____ mg/dl
66. Blood Glucose ____ mg/dl
67. Max VO2 ____ ml/kg/min

Appendix C
Personal Life Cycle

Personal Life Cycle

Life stages

| Protection | Accumulation | Estate planning |

Protection
- Personal independence
- Optimize experiences
- Plans for career, future income
- Select relationships
- Marriage
- Establish lifestyle
- Become parent
- Expand career goals
- Put down roots
- Manage stress of time demands

Accumulation
- Protect personal and family property
- Establish emergency fund
- Insure income with disability and health insurance
- Protect wage-earners with life insurance
- Reevaluate and increase coverages
- Maximize life, disability insurance to protect growing income, estate
- Review insurance to meet anticipated needs
- Adjust life insurance to cover estate taxes, if needed

Estate planning
- Develop budget
- Develop investment philosophy
- Set long-term goals (housing, etc.)
- Handle increased child-rearing costs
- Plan for financing children's education
- Consider investments that minimize taxes
- Establish retirement goals
- More concern with "quality of life"
- Reassess personal priorities and values
- Monitor progress toward financial independence
- Maximize investments
- Budget for retirement lifestyle
- Financial independence

- Start financial recordkeeping system
- Establish relationships with financial advisors
- Make a will
- Revise wills and other legal papers
- Analyze estate plans as children leave home
- Reevaluate estate plan and adjust as needed

Retirement
- Prepare for retirement, expand leisure, community interests
- Adjust to empty nest
- Manage stress of changing relationships and aging process

(This chart represents the most common stages of a working lifetime.)

180

Index

401k plans, 149
403b plans, 149
A. M. Best, 143
Advisors, personal, 126–127
  managing, 127
  selecting, 127
Allen, Woody, 82
American Management Association, The, 13, 61
American Society for Training and Development, 95
Anderson, Nancy, 81
Apprenticeship, 94
Apprenticeship and Training, Bureau of, 93
Armed services, the, 54, 92

Balee, Susan, 12, 14
Bartering, 54
Basic Nutrition and Diet Therapy, 161
Bodner, Joanne, 15
Bolles, Richard N., 72, 95
Business, starting, 26–29
  plan for, 27,
  process of, 27
Business, buying, 42–45
Business, in-home, 42, 57
Business Week, 9, 12, 13, 113

CAD, 83
Care-giving, 54
Careering and Re-careering for the 1990's, 72
CD interactive technology, 83
Chauffeur, 54
Christian, Janet, 161
CNN, 9
COBRA, 140
Consultants
  functions of, 29–30
  reasons for engaging, 30

Consulting
  exploration of, 29–37
  importance of marketing and selling in, 35–36
  models of, 31
  positives and negatives of, 31
  pro bono, 116
  reasons for failure, 37
  skills and knowledge involved, 32–35
Consumer Credit Counseling Service, 138
Contract, working under, 54–55
Corporation, legal form of, 132–135
Courier, 55

Data General, 9
Death, 142
Dell Computer, 17
Disability, 142
Disclosure document, the, 40–41
Do What You Love, the Money Will Follow, 81
Down-scale, 55
Downshifting, 55
Downward mobility, 12

Editor & Publisher Yearbook, 114, 115
Einstein, Albert, 82
Emerson, Ralph Waldo, 1, 3, 19, 63, 97, 125
Employee Assistance Plan, 141
Employment
  alternative, 53–62
  seasonal, 60–61
Employment demand
  by company, 67–68
  by industry type, 66
  by occupation, 68
  by skill, 69
  tables, 68, 69
  by type of knowledge and skill, 69
Employment value, 65–69

Entrepreneurial options, 21
Entrepreneurial personality, 22
  quiz for, 22
Estate planning, 156–157

Financial objectives, 138–139
Five O'Clock Club, The, 121
Flextime, 55
Franchise agreement, 38–39
Franchise Opportunities Handbook, 40
Franchises, 22, 37–42
  description of, 38
  downside of owning, 40
  upside of owning, 39
Franchising Organizations, Directory of, 40

General Electric, 13
General Motors, 13
Geneva Corporation, 61
GI Bill, The, 8
Goodyear, 14
Government, service in, 56
Greger, Janet, 161
Guaranteed investment contracts (GICs),
  149

Hartford Courant, The, 13
Harvard Business School Bulletin, The, 15
Health Reinsurance Association, 140
Health Risk Assessment, 160–161
Health Test, The, 161, 169–177
HMOs, 140
*How to Leave Your Job and Buy a Business
  of Your Own,* 43, 45
*How to Make it Big in the Seminar Busi-
  ness,* 61
Human Resources Information Network, 95

IBM, 14
. Independent contracting, 57–58
  advantages of, 58
  disadvantages of, 58–59
  legal form for, 131
Individual Retirement Accounts, 155
  (*See also* Retirement)
In-placement, 47–50
Insurance, life, 142–143
  rating companies, table, 143
International Franchise Association, 40
Is Coffee Break the Best Part of Your Day?,
  15

Jackson Vocational Interest Survey, 74
Job search
  new strategy for, 103
  techniques of, 99–104
Job Training Programs, Office of, 93
Jones, James Earl, 82

Karasik, Paul, 61
Krannich, Ronald L., 72

Lacey, Dan, 10
Lant, Dr. Jeffrey, 108, 120
Leads groups (*see* Networking)
Leatherman, Dick, 15
Leavy, Dr. Neil B., 16
Legal exposures, 131
Legal form, 131–135
Legal review, 129–130
Legal strategy
  developing, 129–135
  elements of, 130–131
Libraries, 95
Life values, 77–82

Mack, Joseph P., 16
Medicaid, 139, 147, 156, 157
  planning, 156
Medical insurance, 139–142
Medicare, 139, 141
Medigap, 141
Mentors, 94
Modern Nutrition, 161
Moody's, 143
Moonlighting, 59
Mutual Benefit Life, 149
Myers-Briggs Type Indicator, 74
  table of, 75

National Business Employment Weekly, 70
National Health Enhancement Systems, 161,
  170
Network, self-promotion, 122–123
Networking
  care in, 102
  groups, 22
  individual, 121
  new rules of, 102
  objectives of, 103
  old rules of, 102
  targeted audience, 120
New York Times, The, 12, 16, 17

Newsweek, 70
Northeast, 14
Nutrition for Living, 161

Orvis Company, 78
Outplacement, xv, 50–51
Ownership
    four routes to, 25–45
    loneliness in, 25
    pervasiveness of, 25
    risk of, 25

Part-time work, 59
Partnership, 132
Pensions (*see* Retirement planning)
Personal assessment, 71–77
    elements of, 72–76
    limitations of, 76–77
    typical skills in, 73
Personal Financial Planning, 137
Personal service, 59, 60
PPOs, 140
Promotion, self-, 104–123
    objectives for, 108
    techniques of, 108–123
Pryor, Fred, 61

Quoted, becoming, 113–115

Raye-Johnson, Veda, 15
Recruiters, employment, 100, 101, 105
Reebok, 17
Religious service, 59
Retirement
    elements of, 148
    exercises, 151–155
    planning for, 148–156
    risk of inflation in, 152

Saltzman, Amy, 55
Saatchi & Saatchi Advertising, 16
Self-employment, preparing for, 126
Self-initiated performance review (SIPR), 109, 110
Self-promotion matrix, 166–167
Seminar leadership, 61, 117
Shils, Dr. Maurice, 161
Simulation/animation, 83
Sinetar, Marsha, 81
Skills
    acquisition of, 92–96

Skills (*Cont.*):
    hard, 86–89
    mix of, 86
    plan to acquire, 91
    soft, 89–91
Social Security, 149–150
Standard & Poors, 143
Staying Up When Your Job Pulls You Down, 15
Stress, 15
Strong Interest Inventory, 74
    classifications of, table, 75

Tax planning, 156–157
Teaching, 61
Temporary work, 61–62
Three Boxes of Life, The, 72
Tips groups (*see* Networking)
Trade Adjustment Assistance, Office of, 92
Training, on-the-job, 93
Training, work-related, 93–94
Two-Minute Drill, The, 122

U.S. Army, 10
Unabashed Self-Promoter's Guide, The, 108, 120
Unemployment
    preparing for, 126
    protecting against, 144
Unemployment compensation benefits
    calculations of, 146–147
    examples, 145–146
United Way, 147
Uris, Leon, 82

Veterans' Employment and Training Service, 93
Volunteering, 62, 112–113

Wall Street Journal, The, 12, 17, 113
Wealth, accumulation of, 147–148
Wellness, 159–162
Wendleton, Kate, 121
Westinghouse, 14
What Color is Your Parachute?, 72, 95
White House, The, 14
Williams, Sue Rodwell, 161
Work with Passion, 81
Workforce 2000, 68
Workplace Trends, 10
Writers' Market, 114, 115

About the Author

C. D. Peterson is founder and president of Self Reliance Press. As a career expert Peterson has helped thousands with his books, seminars, TV appearances, and personal consultations, using his real-world experience counseling people to create fresh, unique approaches to career survival.

He is a widely respected columnist for *SUCCESS* magazine and the author of two popular books on entrepreneurship: *How to Leave Your Job and Buy a Business of Your Own* and *How to Sell Your Business for More Money in Less Time with Fewer Problems*. A master's degree graduate of MIT's Sloan School of Management, Peterson has held executive positions at such leading firms as International Paper and Merrill Lynch.